Write On!

Quick and Easy Ideas to Motivate Children's Writing

Rachel Kranz

Troll Associates

Interior Illustrations by Shirley Beckes

ISBN: 0-8167-3271-X

Printed in the United States of America.

10 9 8 7 6 5 4 3 2 1

CONTENTS

ACTIVITIES FOR GRADES 3-6

APPENDIX

INTRODUCTION

Writing is one of our most powerful means of communication and expression. That's why it's important that children learn to be good writers. **Write On!** is dedicated to the idea that every student can be a good writer and that every student can enjoy writing. In order to help you achieve these goals in your classroom, this book provides you with inviting activities to motivate your students to write, practical strategies to help them write successfully, and lively reproducible pages to provide them with engaging and meaningful practice. Perhaps most importantly, the activities in **Write On!** are designed to give children the message that, through writing, their thoughts and feelings can have an important impact on other people.

You'll find that each activity starts out by giving students interesting topics to think and write about—topics that are important in their own world. Your young writers will have the chance to write about their families, feelings, and fantasies; to use their senses, their memories, and their imaginations. From writing a recipe for a friend to telling how to clean up pollution...from imagining an adventure under the sea to describing the things that make them mad, **Write On!** offers students topics that will motivate them to write by capturing their interest.

You'll also notice that the activities are geared toward showing your students that writing is not a meaningless task, but a real-life activity with a specific purpose: to describe, inform, explore feelings, share ideas, entertain, or accomplish some other important goal. Moreover, each activity stresses that students are writing for a real audience—actual people who will read and react to what they have to say. And they'll learn and practice strategies for gearing their writing to a specific purpose and audience—strategies like using concrete details, creating vivid images, using rich sensory language, choosing precise words, presenting clear and coherent arguments, structuring a story, creating interesting characters, and writing lively, believable dialogue.

In addition to providing plenty of meaningful and motivating topics, **Write On!** gives students the opportunity to choose from a wide variety of genres to best suit the ideas and feelings they want to communicate. Your students will grow to understand that a genre is not chosen arbitrarily for the sake of an "assignment," but because it provides the best means of communicating in a particular way. Students will experiment with a number of different genres: letters, poems, fantasies, autobiographies, memoirs, editorials, science reports, greeting card messages, and many more.

How This Book Is Organized

Write On! begins with activities geared toward writers in grades K-2. These first forays into writing focus on ideas and experiences that young children can relate to, although older students may enjoy them as well. The second half of the book includes activities of special interest to students in grades 3-6.

As you can see from the Table of Contents, the activities are grouped in thematic units. Each unit begins with a teacher's page that provides ways of drawing children into the theme, strategies to help them write about the theme, and suggestions for working with the reproducible students' pages that follow. The activities in each unit are designed to build on each other and can be used sequentially, but they can also be used separately if you prefer.

Most of the writing activities in **Write On!** can be done by individuals, partners, small groups, or, occasionally, the whole class. Sometimes the teacher's page will make suggestions in this regard; sometimes the reproducible page will mention a partner or a group. In any case, feel free to adapt activities to suit your needs and those of your students. Feel free, as well, to adapt any of the suggestions or activities in this book to the needs of your class or of a particular student.

The more skill and confidence a writer develops, the greater the chances of finding joy in writing. The ideas and activities in this book can help you guide your students to achieve their own sense of mastery and pleasure in the process of writing as well as pride and satisfaction in their finished products.

WRITE ON!

INTRODUCTION TO GRADES K-2

While primary-grade children are beginning writers, they are already highly skilled communicators. They take great pleasure in the spoken word and have no trouble expressing complex ideas, feelings, and fantasies in spoken language. The first section of **Write On!** taps into young children's natural enthusiasm for spoken language to create excitement about writing.

The early activities introduce young children to writing by drawing on feelings and experiences they can talk about easily. Why does this section start with the five senses? Because it's the basic way young children experience their world. Sections on holidays, families, friends, food, and feelings give your students a chance to explore, through writing, the familiar world in which they feel confident and comfortable. In these activities students will begin to flex their writing muscles by employing sense words, writing simple sentences, stringing sentences together to describe an event, picture, or idea, composing poems, and suggesting titles for pictures.

In later activities students will expand the range of their writing as they explore playing with words, storytelling, and diary writing. In "Story Time," for example, they'll learn the rudiments of storytelling—creating characters, dialogue, and story structure. They'll also get a chance to use a wonderful piece of children's literature as a model for their writing—Taro Yashima's *Crow Boy*. (If you like, you can adapt the activity to another literature selection.) At the end of this section, you'll find some ideas for showing your students how to make their own books—an exciting activity they can do by themselves, with partners, or as a class.

All the activities in this first section of **Write On!** are geared to show children that writing can be fun and meaningful and to help them achieve a sense of mastery and confidence with written communication.

Our Five Senses

Some of the best writing material can come right from your students' own five senses. These classroom games—and the reproducibles on pages 10-15—can help your students sharpen their senses and "open their eyes" to a whole new world of ideas for writing. These activities also provide lots of practice with sensory words to help your students' **descriptive writing** come alive!

Look Around

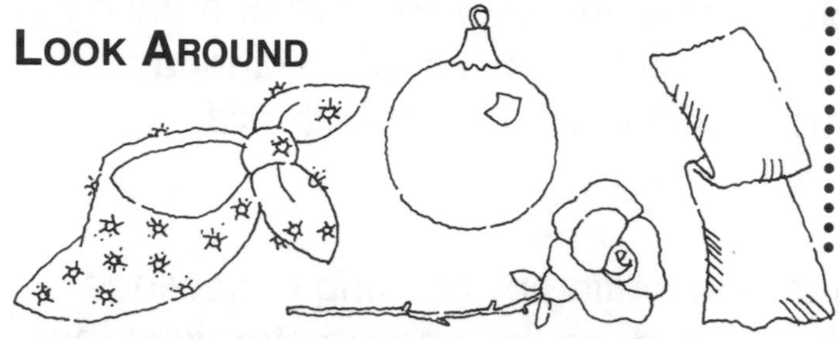

Here are two games to help children prepare for "Look Around" on page 10.

Name That Thing!

Materials: Unusual-looking objects, such as a sparkly scarf, a shiny ornament, a bright red rose, a crumbling, worn piece of leather

Hold up each item and ask the children to name it. Write the name of each object on the chalkboard. Next, ask the children to suggest descriptive sight words for each object, and list their words on the chalkboard. Finally, cover the names of the objects and see if the children can identify each one just by the descriptive words.

I Spy

One child says, "I spy, with my little eye, something that is ______."

The child should keep adding sight words until someone guesses what the object is. (Make sure that your players are choosing objects that everyone can see!)

Listen Up

This game will give your class some practice in describing sounds. It's a good warm-up for "Listen Up," the reproducible on page 11, where they'll write about a sound that they enjoy.

The Joys of Noise

Materials: Noisemakers such as party horns, a whistle, a coffee can full of pebbles, a glass bottle full of water, a spoon to tap against the bottle, two spoons to hit together

Invite the children to take turns making different kinds of sounds with noisemakers or with their voices; for example, animal sounds, traffic sounds, or sounds they hear in school. Encourage the rest of the class to contribute words that describe each sound. Write the words on the chalkboard. Then challenge other children to repeat the sounds their classmates made as you point to each group of words. Did the precise descriptions help them remember the sounds?

Tasty Times

How do you describe a taste? This game can help your class find out and will provide lots of taste words to use in their **descriptive writing.**

Taste Tests

Materials: Lots of different-tasting and different-textured foods in containers that hide the food (Make sure no one has any food allergies!)

Let each child taste one of the foods without seeing it. Invite the tasters to suggest descriptive words—salty, sticky, sweet, crunchy, spicy—to see if the rest of the class can guess the food.

With the descriptions of these foods fresh in their minds, get them started on "Tasty Times," the reproducible on page 12.

Sweet and Bitter

Good writers evoke moods or feelings by using words that appeal to *all* the senses, including the sense of smell. The following activities will help students to improve their writing by getting them to "think with their noses!"

I Smell Something...

Have a child think of a place with a distinctive smell—the beach, a new car, a basement—and describe the smell only. ("I am smelling salty seaweed. I am smelling delicious hot dogs.") Can students guess the place by smell alone? You might want to play this game in "smelling teams," with small groups agreeing on a "smelling" place and calling out descriptions together. Now that they've generated lots of smell words, they're all warmed up for "Sweet and Bitter," the reproducible on page 13.

Getting in Touch

Need some good words to describe the feel of things? Play this game with your class before they work on "Getting in Touch," the reproducible on page 14. It will help students stretch their vocabularies by describing objects using touch words.

Touchy, Touchy

Materials: A "touchy box"—a shoe box with a small opening cut into the lid; a variety of things to feel—velvet, a glass marble, Velcro, burlap, a lemon

Let students close their eyes and feel an object in the "touchy box." Invite them to write down some touch words and then guess what they touched, or let them work in pairs to share their words and guesses. Show everyone all the objects. Can they pick out the ones they touched? (One variation on this game is to let students close their eyes and touch objects with their elbows, forearms, or knees.)

Making Sense

Brainstorm a wall full of sense words by making a chart on the chalkboard with a column for each of the five senses. Now when students start their stories for "Making Sense," the reproducible on page 15, they'll have the words they need "at their fingertips!"

Name ______________________________ Date ______________

Look Around

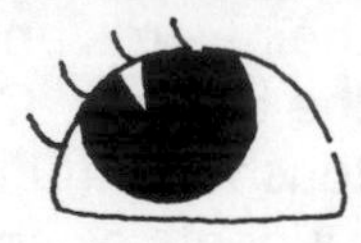
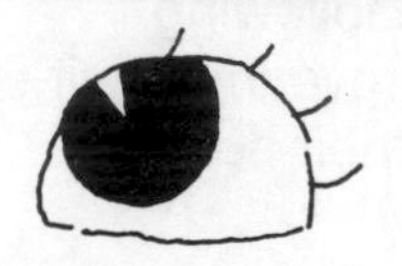

Look around the room you are in.
Find something that you like to look at.
Draw a picture of it. Then write about what you see.

____

____

____

____

____

____

Name ______________________________ Date ________________

LISTEN UP

Crash! Ting-a-ling! Clang! Woof! Grrr! Bzzz!
Think of a sound that you like. Draw a picture of someone or something making that sound. Then write about your picture. Tell how the sound makes you feel.

____

____

____

____

____

____

Name ________________________________ Date ________________

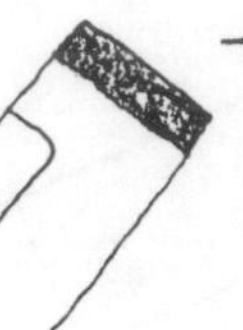

Tasty Times

Mmmm! Some foods taste good! **Yuck!** Some foods taste awful! Draw three foods you love and three foods you don't like at all. Then write one or more taste words next to each food.

Tastes I Love | **Taste Words**

1. ____________________
____

2. ____________________
____

3. ____________________
____

Tastes I Don't Like

1. ____________________
____

2. ____________________
____

3. ____________________
____

Name ______________________________ Date ______________

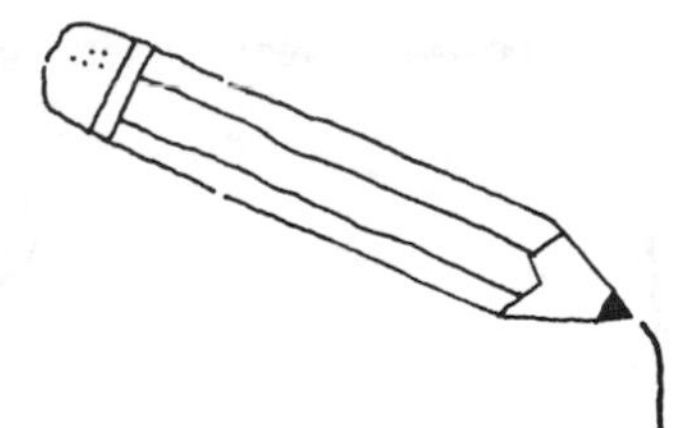

Sweet and Bitter

This NOSE-Y detective is confused. He is smelling two things at once—one is sweet, the other is bitter. Help him out! Think of two things he could be smelling. Draw a picture of each thing he smells. Then write a story about the two smells. Tell how the detective found out what they were.

Draw something sweet.

Draw something bitter.

____

____

____

____

____

____

Name ____ Date ____________________

Getting in Touch

Touchy Tom can't look in—he can only feel with his paw! Draw a picture of what Tom thinks he touched. Then write about what it felt like.

Here are some touch words to help you when you write:

fluffy slimy rough cold silky wet bumpy round pointy

____

____

____

____

____

____

Name ______________________________ Date ______________

Making Sense

Look at the picture. Then finish the story.

Once upon a time, there were five animal friends. The raccoon had special eyes. The fox had special ears. The dog had a special nose that could smell anything, near or far. The monkey could touch things and tell what they were, even in the dark. And the rabbit had a special mouth that made everything taste sweet!

One day, the five friends were out walking when ______________________________

____

____

____

____

____

____

____

Holidays: A Time for Giving

Sharing holiday customs and traditions provides fabulous writing opportunities for personal narratives, **how-to writing**, and even poems and songs. The reproducibles on pages 17-20 are just a few of the possibilities for holiday writing.

A New Holiday

The reproducible, "A New Holiday," on page 17 gives children a chance to experiment with **how-to writing** as they invent their very own holiday. You might help them get started by asking questions like:

- Can you name some holidays?
- What's your favorite holiday?
- Why is that holiday special to you?
- What do you like to do on that day?

Holiday Greeting Card

If you could invent your own holiday, what kind of card would go with it? Your students can design their own cards in "Holiday Greeting Card," the reproducible on page 18.

You and your class might enjoy sharing a wide variety of greeting cards from your homes before students start designing their own.

Cut out the pattern and fold it in half on the center line. Show children how to draw a picture on the front of the card. Then show them how to open the card and decorate it. Encourage them to write a message inside to try their hands at writing a note or writing a **short poem.**

The Perfect Gift

Ask your students what they would choose if they could have *any* present in the whole world. You might get them started with suggestions like "a pencil that would do all my homework for me" or "a bicycle that could fly." List their suggestions on the chalkboard or on chart paper, so they'll have a great list to refer to when they do some **descriptive writing** about "The Perfect Gift" (page 19).

Giving a Present

Why do we give presents? Is it fun to give presents *and* to get them? Use these questions as springboards for your class to share stories about giving and getting presents. Then wonder along with the children, "If I could give any present I wanted to anyone in the world, what would I do?" Now they're all warmed up for the **narrative writing** in "Giving a Present" (page 20).

Name ______________________________ Date ______________

A New Holiday

Invent a new holiday! Tell when the holiday happens and what it is for. Then tell how people would celebrate it. You can also make a greeting card for your new holiday. Give your holiday card to a friend, a family member, or a neighbor.

Holiday Greeting Card

Cut out the card shape. Fold the card on the dotted line. On the front, draw a picture that shows something about your new holiday. Inside, write a message that tells something about your new holiday. You can draw a picture on the inside, too.

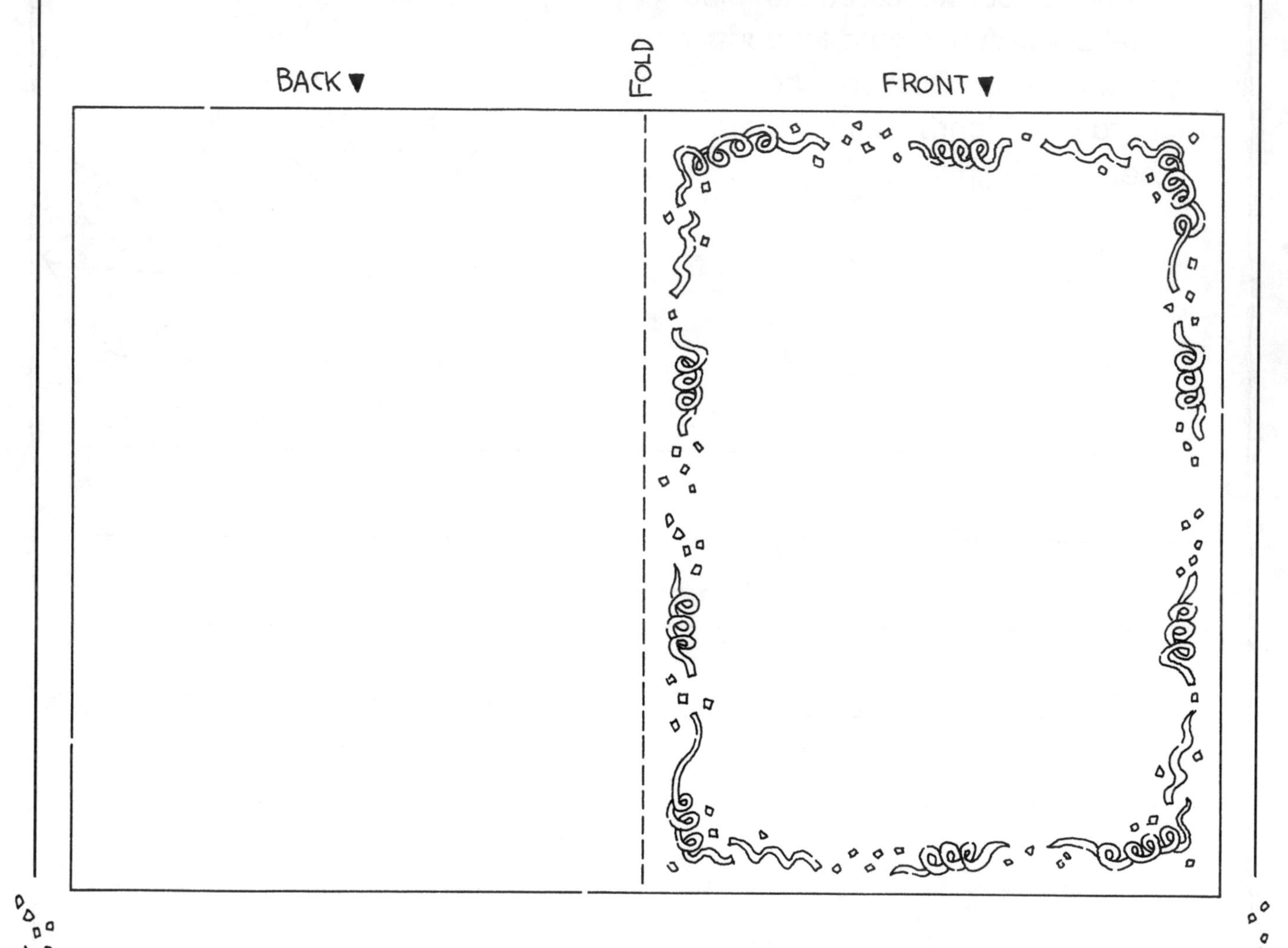

Name ______________________ Date ____________

The Perfect Gift

What do you think is in the box? It's the present you want most in the whole world! Draw the present inside the box. It can be real or make believe. Then write all about your wonderful present and the person who gave it to you.

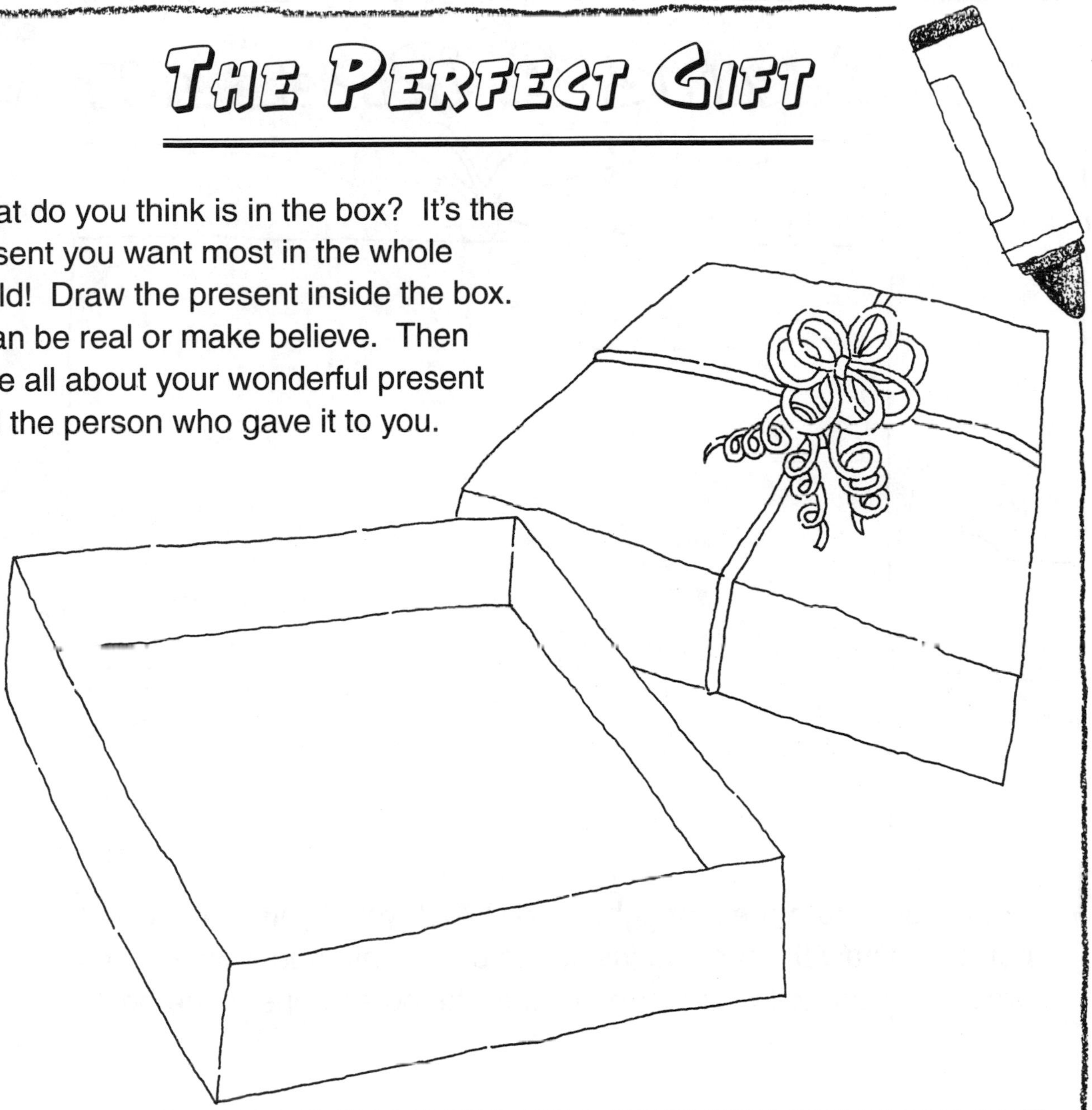

Name ______________________________ Date ______________

Who could use a present right now? What would you like to give that person? Draw the present inside the box. Write about who is getting the present. Then tell what happens after the person opens the box!

____

____

____

____

____

____

FAMILIES

Children write best when they're writing about what they know. And what do they know most about? Most often, it's the people around them—their families.

FAMILY PICTURES

Help children think about families by asking questions such as:

- What is a family?
- Can pets be part of a family?
- What are some things families do together?
- What are some things you like to do with your family?

While they're thinking about families, give the children a chance to write **personal narratives** about their families in "Family Pictures" (page 22).

FAMILY TIME

Young writers sometimes like to talk about their topics first. Then they're bursting with ideas when they face the page. Invite your students to talk about what their families do at different times of the day to warm them up for the **autobiographical writing** in "Family Time," the reproducible on page 23. A way to help them focus on the topic would be to show a model of a clock. As you move the hands around (or draw different times on the chalkboard) ask, "What do you do with your family at this time of day?" Then let them choose their favorite times to write about.

Name ______________________ Date ______________

This frame is for a picture of your family. Draw something you did together. Then write about what you did. Tell why it was special to you.

____

____

____

____

____

____

Name ______________________________ Date ____________________

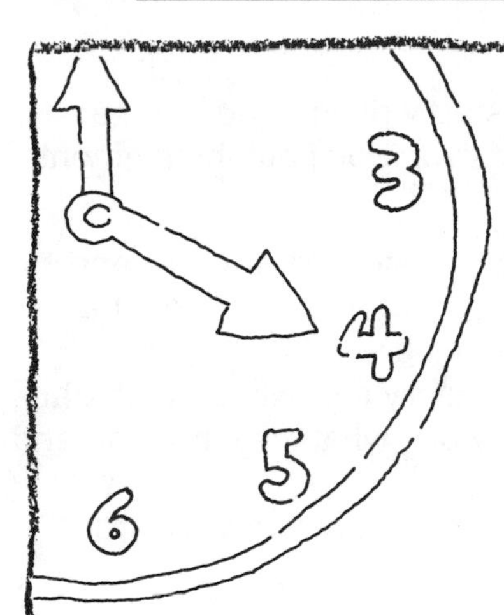

FAMILY TIME

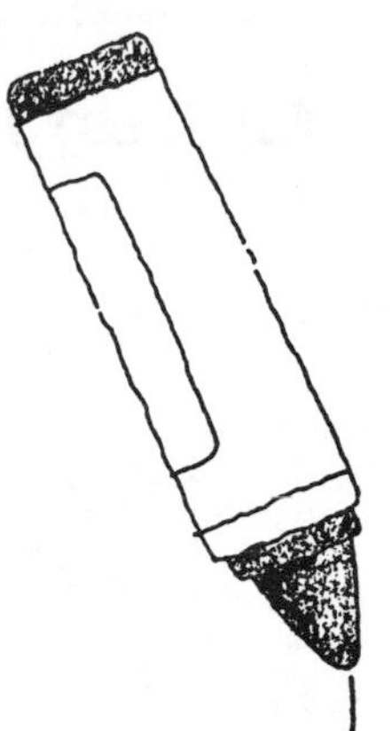

What's your favorite time of day with your family? Is it the morning? Dinnertime? Bedtime? Draw a picture of what you and your family do at that favorite time. Then write all about what you do.

____

____

____

____

____

____

FRIENDS

MY BEST FRIEND

In "My Best Friend" on page 25, children write a **poem** about friendship. Ease them into this activity by helping them think about both friends and poetry. To focus on friends, ask questions such as:

- What is a friend?
- Why do we need friends?
- What are some things friends do together?
- Can an animal be your friend?

Share with the class some poems about friendship, or have volunteers read some poems aloud. Your students might enjoy poetry by Eve Merriam, Langston Hughes, and Gwendolyn Brooks.

A FIGHT WITH A FRIEND

In "A Fight with a Friend" on page 26, children have the chance to write a **short story**. Help them connect to what they know by inviting students to tell about times that they had a fight with a friend and made up afterwards.

Before children start writing, read them a short fairy tale or fable. Point out the elements of a story:

- The beginning of a story tells where and when the story takes place. It tells who the characters in the story are.
- The middle of a story tells what the characters said, what they did, what they thought, and how they felt.
- The end of a story tells how everything turned out.

This would be a good time to introduce quotation marks and dialogue, if you feel your class is ready.

ADVENTURE WITH A FRIEND

Children love adventure play, and they'll enjoy the chance to write an **adventure story** of their own. Get them started by asking "What is an adventure?" and encourage children to share some adventure stories they have read or have seen on television or at the movies.

You might ask questions such as:

- If you could have any adventure you wanted, where would you go?
- Who would go with you? Would that person be real or imaginary?
- What would you do together?

Then give your students "Adventure with a Friend" (page 27) and let them take off!

Name ______________________________ Date ______________

MY BEST FRIEND

Who is your best friend? Write a poem about that person. Start each line with a letter from the word FRIEND. In your poem, you could tell what is special about your friend.

F ______________________________

R ______________________________

I ______________________________

E ______________________________

N ______________________________

D ______________________________

You might want to give the poem to your friend to read.

Name ______________________________ Date ______________

A Fight With A Friend

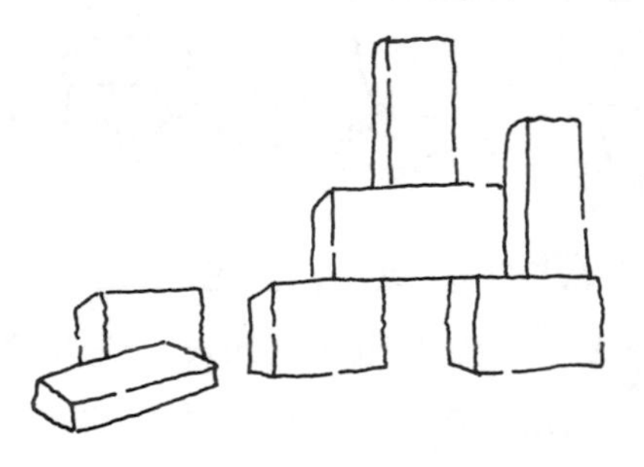

Two friends are having a fight. Draw the two friends. Then write about the fight. Be sure to tell how they made up afterward.

____

____

____

____

____

____

Name ______________________________ Date ____________

Adventure With A Friend

Once upon a time, two friends went on a big adventure. Draw a picture of something the two friends did. Then write a story about their whole adventure.

____

____

____

____

____

____

Food Fun

What goes together like peanut butter and jelly? Children and food! They sing about it, make faces at it, and love to write about it. The reproducibles on pages 29-31 can lead to very delectable results.

The Most Delicious Meal in the World

Sometimes writing about food can be almost as much fun as eating it! Help children discover the joys of **descriptive writing** about food in "The Most Delicious Meal in the World" (page 29).

Get them started by inviting them to talk about favorite foods and tastes (sweet, salty, crunchy) as you write the words on the chalkboard or on chart paper. Invite them to invent some foods, like a pizza topped with peanut butter and jelly or a drink made with one hundred strawberries mixed with orange juice. While their imaginations are cooking, they can start writing!

Yuck!

Nobody likes to eat yucky food, but sometimes it's fun to write about. Children can enjoy **writing descriptions** of the worst food in the world for "Yuck!," the reproducible on page 30.

Get students going by listing descriptions of food they dislike on the chalkboard. You might ask, "Can some people dislike a food and other people like it?" Help them make their descriptions specific by encouraging them to tell *why* they don't like a food—it's slimy or sticky, mushy or bitter—and list those words on the chalkboard. Then invite the students to invent some yucky food combinations. Remind them to use the notes on the board for inspiration.

Cooking Up a Storm

Children can have fun with **how-to writing** in "Cooking Up a Storm," the reproducible on page 31. Help prepare them by discussing what a recipe is. You might enjoy sharing some real recipe cards or cookbooks with the children, or invite them to bring some in from home. Children also might enjoy sharing some of their own cooking experiences.

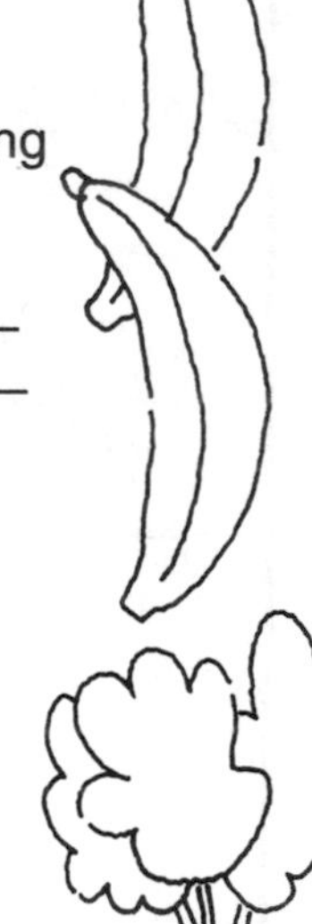

Then tell students that they are going to write a recipe for something we *don't* eat—a storm! Invite them to brainstorm different kinds of storms—wind, rain, snow, hurricane, tornado—and list them on the chalkboard.

Help them think about storm elements by asking:

- How can you tell a storm is coming?
- What happens during a storm?
- What is the end of a storm like?

Your students might appreciate a model from you ("Take one huge wind and blow hard through all the streets. Then add some loud thunder and bright lightning...") before they start cooking up their own storms.

Name ______________________________ Date ______________

The Most Delicious Meal In The World

On this table is the most delicious meal ever! It may have foods you have tasted or foods you are inventing. Draw the foods. Then tell about how they taste, feel, and smell.

____

____

____

____

____

____

Name ________________________________ Date ______________

Yuck!

On this table are foods you don't like. Draw pictures of them. Then tell what they are. Tell how they look, taste, feel, and smell.

____

____

____

____

____

____

Name ______________________________ Date ______________

COOKING UP A STORM

What is the recipe for a storm? In part 1, name some things in a storm. In part 2, tell what happens in the storm.

Ingredients

____

____

____

____

____

____

Directions

____

____

____

____

____

____

Feelings

To help the children use **personal narratives** to write about feelings, you might want to ask some questions:

- What are some different feelings that we have?
- How do you know when someone is angry?
- How do you know when someone is happy?
- How do people act when they are sad?
- Can you have two feelings at the same time? How?

Then ask children to think about how they feel inside when they have these different feelings. Can they use pictures to tell how they feel? Encourage them to talk about their feelings and how they can show them. The reproducibles on pages 33, 34, and 35 will give students practice using **expressive language**.

Things That Make Me Angry

Invite children to think of some things that make them angry, and list the words on the chalkboard. Encourage them to be very specific and give lots of detail. You might prompt them with such suggestions as, "I really get angry about itchy clothes that scratch my neck!" or "It makes me so angry when someone pushes in front of me on line!"

My Favorite Things

Ask children to think about times when they are happy. Encourage them to talk about some of the things that are part of those happy times, such as places, people, animals, and food. Then ask, "Does everybody feel happy about the same things?"

Being Sad

Ask children to name some experiences that might make people sad. You might suggest things like a favorite toy breaking or having a friend who can't come to play. Encourage children to talk about how they feel inside when they are sad and to use pictures to describe how they feel. Then read them some poetry about sadness. Invite them to share their reactions to the poems before writing their own **poems**.

Name ____________________ Date ____________

Things That Make Me Angry

What really makes you angry? Draw something that makes you feel this way. Write about how you feel.

Name ______________________________ Date ______________

My Favorite Things

This room is full of your favorite things. What are they? Draw pictures of some of them. Then write about why you love them.

____

____

____

____

____

____

Name ______________________________ Date ________________

BEING SAD

What makes you sad?
Write a poem about a sad thing that happened. Tell how it made you feel inside.

Fun With Words

Good writers know that words are their building blocks. Having a feel for words—how they sound, how they are put together, their sometimes unexpected meanings—is essential for anyone who wants to write well.

The reproducibles on pages 37-38 will help your students use words with more freedom and playfulness. As they build their **vocabulary**, **word choice**, and **word/sound skills**, they'll also have fun and gain greater confidence in their ability to work and play with the building blocks of writing.

Rhyme Time

Even very young students can rhyme simple words, which gives them a sense of power and mastery as they use language. "Rhyme Time," the reproducible on page 37, helps students increase their **awareness of words** and is also a good preparation for writing **rhyming poetry**.

Before handing out the reproducible, have some rhyming fun with your students. Write a word on the chalkboard and invite them to contribute words that rhyme with it. Some words you might find especially rhyme-friendly:

book	**stick**	**may**
house	**far**	**see**

You might want to leave these words on the board to help students as they complete the reproducible.

Then challenge your students to use as many rhyming words as possible in a single sentence; for example, "I *took* a *look* for my favorite *book* but stopped to *cook* some Jell-O that *shook*." This practice will help them complete the reproducible—and will give them an appreciation for the way good writers pay attention to word sounds as well as to word meanings.

The Word Makers

One of the best ways for children to feel that they are "masters of the language" is to let them make up their own words. Inventing words and definitions for "The Word Makers," the reproducible on page 38, will help them build the **vocabulary skills** essential to any good writer.

You might get students started by inviting them to suggest some known words and definitions, and writing them on the chalkboard. Then tell them you are going to make up some words and definitions and example sentences:

"**Milkwich**—a sandwich and milk snack. I had a milkwich after school today."

"**Gleep**—the gurgling noise that sheep make when they drink water too fast. The thirsty sheep made a loud gleep."

Let them try inventing a few words—and when they've got the hang of it, on to the reproducible!

Name ______________________________ Date ________________

Rhyme Time

True

Moo

Shoe

These rhyming words have gotten all mixed up! Put each one in the right place. Then, write some rhyming words on the lines below.

stick	**may**	**see**
________	________	________
________	________	________

Just for Fun: Write a sentence. Use as many rhyming words as you can.

____

____

____

Name ______________________ Date ______________

Mewp!

The Word Makers

munchgum!

You can invent some words of your own! Write three new words on the left side. On the right side, tell what the words mean. Then draw a picture for each word.

New Word	What It Means	Drawing
1. ______	______ ______	
2. ______	______ ______	
3. ______	______ ______	

gleep!

Just for Fun: Now show how to use your new words. Write each one in a sentence.

Milkwich!

1. ______________________________

2. ______________________________

3. ______________________________

Story Time

The reproducibles on pages 40-43 will introduce your students to the elements of **short stories—characters**, **dialogue**, and **story structure**. Children will also get to use Taro Yashima's sensitive story, *Crow Boy*, as a model for their own writing.

Start by inviting students to bring in their own favorite books to share. Encourage them to tell the stories to the class to get a feel for what's needed to make a story clear and interesting.

What Do You See?

Crow Boy, by acclaimed children's author and illustrator Taro Yashima, tells of a shy little boy who wins respect and recognition from his classmates for his remarkable knowledge of nature. This sensitive tale provides an excellent example of **realistic fiction** on which students might model their own writing. Read the book aloud. Can the students recall the animals and plants that Chibi observes and learns about? Point out that they probably remember them because the author has given us so many specific and vivid details.

Invite the children to contribute their own specific observations of nature by completing the reproducible on page 40, "What Do You See?" Explain that close observation of the world around us helps us to make the world we write about real to our readers.

Story People

Get your class thinking about **characters** by answering the questions in "Story People," the reproducible on page 41. Start by using one or two characters that they all know—perhaps including Chibi from *Crow Boy* or a real person. Then give students the reproducible. Answering these questions about their own story people will give students the building blocks for creating interesting and recognizable characters.

Talking Up a Storm

Your young writers can work in pairs to complete "Talking Up a Storm," the reproducible on page 42. Let each student take the part of one of the characters. (If necessary, you can change some characters to Speedy Samantha and Officer Oliver!) Invite them to talk through the conversation first, then write down what they said. This will help them write vivid, playful, natural-sounding **dialogue**. Your class will also enjoy seeing some dialogues acted out.

Beginning, Middle, End

"Beginning, Middle, End," the reproducible on page 43, will help your students identify the elements of **story structure**, so that they can eventually create well-organized and satisfying tales of their own. You might warm students up by working as a class to answer the reproducible's questions, using one or two stories that they all know. Then invite students to make up some answers for their own stories. Students might enjoy working in small groups to complete this project.

Name ______________________________ Date ______________

What Do You See?

When Chibi in *Crow Boy* looks around, he sees beautiful things in nature that other people don't seem to notice. Look out of a window to find something beautiful. Draw it in the window on this page. Then write about what you see.

____

____

____

____

____

Name ______________________________ Date ______________

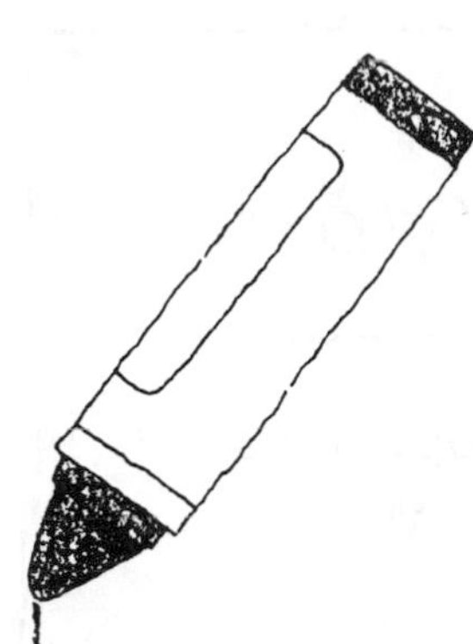

STORY PEOPLE

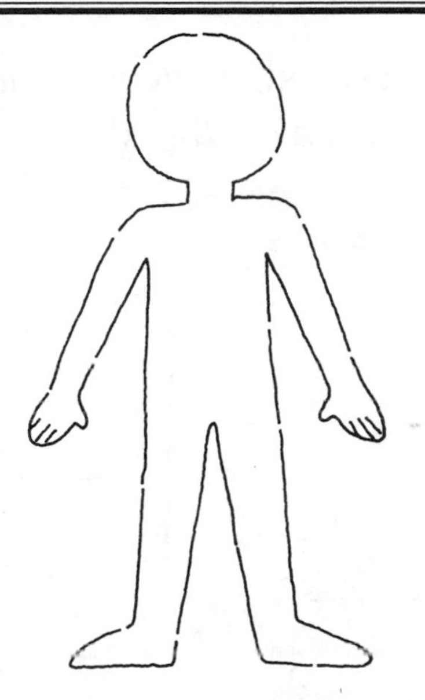

Every story is about someone. Whom would you like to write about? Finish the picture of the person in the space above. Then complete these sentences. Later, write your story.

My character's name is ______________________________.

My character lives in ______________________________

______________________________.

My character likes ______________________________

______________________________.

My character doesn't like ______________________________

______________________________.

My character is different because ______________________________

______________________________.

Name ______________________________ Date ______________

Talking up a Storm

Speedy Sam was going too fast! Officer Olivia made him stop. What does Sam say to Officer Olivia? What does she say to him? Write what they said.

Name ______________________________ Date ____________________

Every story has a beginning, a middle, and an end.
Think of a story you want to tell.
Then complete the sentences below. Later, write your story.

Beginning

My story takes place in ______________________.

The two main characters are:

1. ____________________________________

2. ____________________________________

The story starts when ________________________

____.

Middle

The next thing that happens is _________________

____.

Then,_______________________________________

____.

End

At the end,___________________________________.

DIARIES

MY DIARY

Before your young diarists start writing their own daily records, share the following list with them by writing it on the chalkboard:

Things That Can Be in a Diary

- memories
- thoughts
- feelings
- wishes
- hopes
- dreams
- pictures and drawings
- a description of a day's events

Introduce your students to the pleasures of **diary writing** by letting your class write a group diary. At the end of the day, write student suggestions on the board to create a record of interesting, funny, or sad things that happened that day.

You might also want to model a diary page that you yourself write, including some personal thoughts and feelings. For example:

Dear Diary,

Today the class and I took a fascinating field trip to Redwood Forest. The trees have the most beautiful bark—exactly the same color as the fur on my Irish setter. I was amazed to see how tall the trees were. It hurt my neck to look up at something so high! It felt so good to stand in their deep, dark shade, after walking in the hot sun. I wonder how old they are—and how many years they will still be standing.

After the trip was over, I felt tired but happy. I can't wait to go back there again! Maybe one summer I can spend some time studying more about those interesting trees.

You might want to give each student several copies of "My Diary," the reproducible on page 45. Then help them fasten the pages together with string, yarn, or metal fasteners. You can either review their diaries at the end of the year or allow the children to keep their writing private.

YOU CHOOSE

Young writers feel empowered and excited when they get to choose their own topics, as in "You Choose," the reproducible on page 46. Remind your students that they'll have the most fun writing about something that interests them. A helpful hint: Students might want to picture telling their writing to an ideal audience—a friend, parent, or other relative. As they imagine what this interested and supportive person wants to hear, they'll find words and ideas flowing more easily. After the writing is done, students might enjoy reading their work aloud to writing partners, small writing groups, or the whole class.

Name ______________________________ Date ____________________

My Diary

Something interesting that happened today

____

____

____

____

Something funny that happened today

____

____

____

____

Something sad that happened today

____

____

____

____

Name ______________________ Date ____________

You Choose

Choose your own topic! You can write about anything you want.

This "Writing Well" might give you some ideas.

Dinosaurs
If I Ruled the World
Dinner Time
My Aunt
My Favorite Place
The Talking Dog and the Singing Cat

Making Books

Making books can be a wonderful small-group or whole-class project. Making their own books helps students approach writing with confidence.

On pages 48 and 49, we've included models for two books, a "How-To Book" (for older or more advanced students) and "Things to Wear" (for younger or less advanced students). Duplicate the reproducibles and allow each class member to complete a page and cut out its outline. Then use oaktag, construction paper, or some other stiff paper to make a front and back cover, to be decorated by one or more students. Use yarn, string, or brass fasteners to bind the books.

You can also use this format to create other group books. For example:

- "Our Circus Book," with pages shaped like clowns and featuring circus scenes
- "Day Dreams and Night Dreams," with cloud-shaped pages. Students can draw the pictures they see in clouds, or dream images
- "An Alphabet Book," with each page in the shape of a different letter
- "The Beach Book," with pages shaped like blazing suns, featuring beach scenes
- "Tales of Whales," with whale-shaped pages and underwater scenes
- "Shopping Stories," with shopping-basket-shaped pages showing and telling about things we do at the store
- "Our Recipe Book," with cake-shaped pages for recipes
- "Horse Tales," with horse-head pages and horsey scenes
- "The Earth Book," with pages shaped like a globe, full of ideas for cleaning up pollution or protecting the earth
- "The Book of Friends," with pages shaped like a person's figure, telling about friendship and things friends do together.

A How-To Book

To complete "A How-To Book," the reproducible on page 48, give each student a copy of the page. Help students identify the key elements of **how-to writing**—being clear and giving information in an order that makes sense. To prepare, you could model a how-to explanation yourself, or ask students to explain how to do something, such as tie a shoe, cook pudding, or make a bed.

Things to Wear

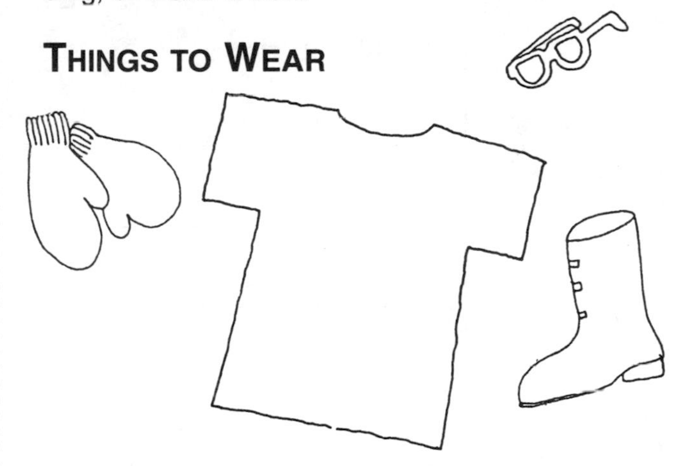

Invite your class to brainstorm a list of things to wear. Then encourage each student to choose which one he or she wants to draw and write about, using the reproducible on page 49. This picture book can be a whole–class or a small–group project.

A How-To Book

Cut out the page. Draw a picture of something you know how to make. Then write instructions for making the thing you drew.

Your teacher will put your page together with your classmates' to make a class how-to book.

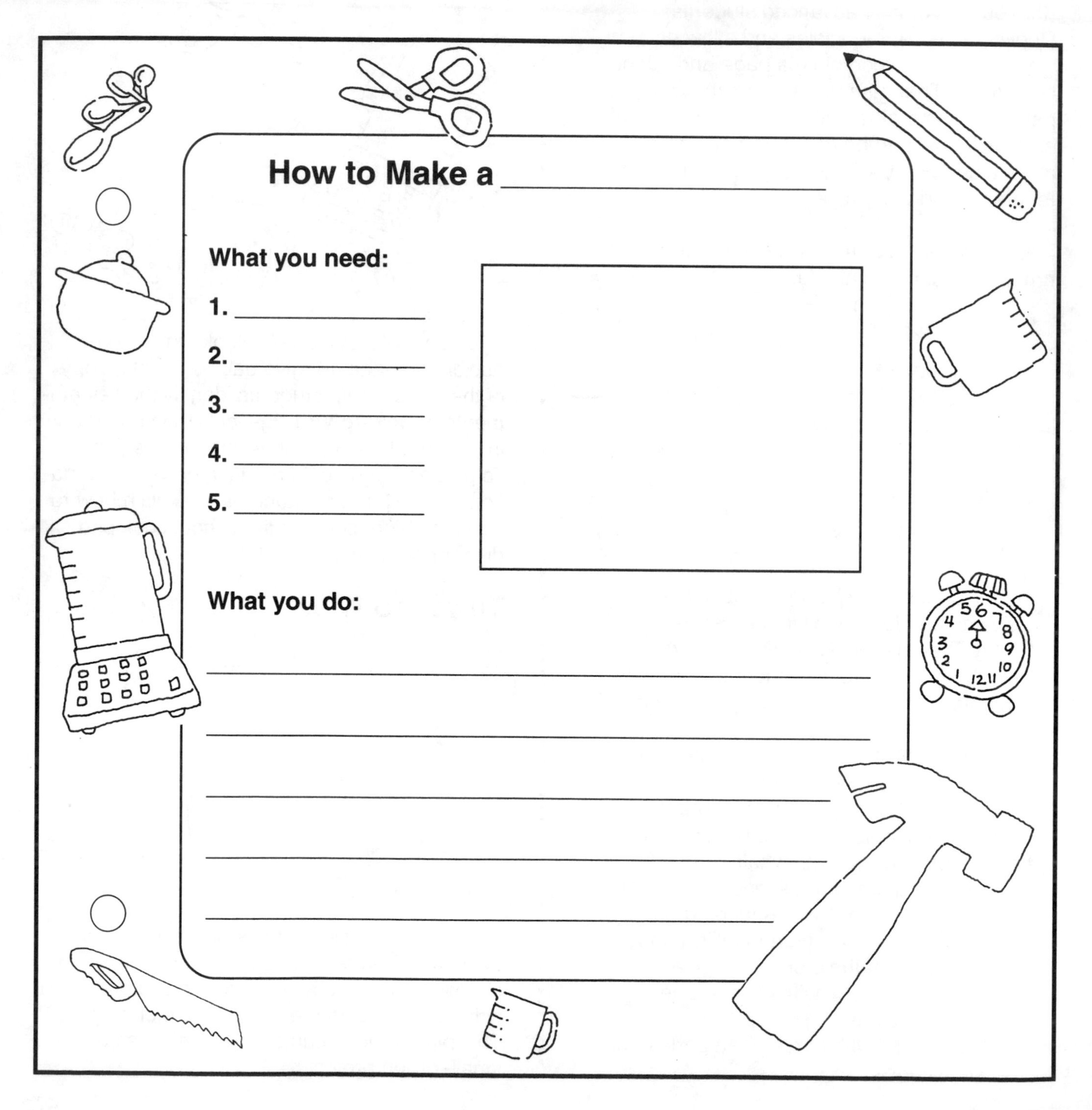

How to Make a ____________________

What you need:

1. ____________
2. ____________
3. ____________
4. ____________
5. ____________

What you do:

____

____

____

____

____

Things To Wear

Cut out the page. Draw a picture of something you like to wear. Then write about what it looks like and why you like to wear it.

Your teacher will put your page together with your classmates' to make a class book about things to wear.

Introduction to Grades 3-6

Children in the intermediate grades enjoy a sense of increased mastery in their writing. At this level, they are writing longer, more complex sentences, combining sentence elements, varying sentence structure, and beginning to use figurative language, as well as expressing more complex and abstract ideas. In addition, they are learning to spell accurately and follow the basic rules of grammar, usage, and punctuation.

While you may find many writing activities from the first section of this book adaptable for your intermediate-grade class, this section of **Write On!** gives students in grades 3-6 the opportunity to use their newly developed skills to write in a wide variety of genres about topics older children think and feel strongly about. They'll write descriptions, stories, letters, reports, speeches, dialogue, poems, and riddles.

In addition, they'll be encouraged to communicate ideas, opinions, and feelings about topics that range from friends and family, to adventure stories, to the world we live in.

The activities in this section of **Write On!** will appeal to your students' sense of fun, mixing plenty of creativity and imagination with the factual and the personal. "Myself" (pages 51-54) invites students to describe themselves both as they are and as they would like to be; in "The People I Know'' (pages 55-59), children will write about their family histories, think about what makes a real friend, and think about people they'd choose for company on a desert island; "Telling Tales" (pages 82-85), gives your students the chance to respond to the moving story, "Slower than the Rest," from Cynthia Rylant's *Every Living Thing*, and offers three reproducibles that teach the basic rudiments of short-story writing; "Diaries and Journals" (pages 86-88) includes a diary page that can be duplicated and bound so that children can make their own personal books.

Your intermediate-grade students are thinking about more complex topics and expressing themselves in more sophisticated ways. They'll enjoy exercising a new, wider range of writing options in this section of **Write On!**

MYSELF

Your students will enjoy creating **descriptions** and **personal narratives** in the reproducibles on pages 52-54. Concentrating on themselves—a topic on which they are unquestionably the experts—will help students develop a sense of ownership and authority in their writing.

WHO I AM

Students get a chance to polish their **descriptive writing** skills in "Who I Am," on page 52. They'll get good practice in using concrete details and examples, as well as preparation for creating interesting fictional characters and writing vivid news and feature stories.

Start by encouraging your class to describe a person they all know—perhaps even you! You might use the prompts on the reproducible to get started. Then discuss what makes a good description. What kinds of details, imagery, and examples make a person come alive?

With these elements in mind, your students are now all warmed up to complete the reproducible.

MY DREAM SELF

Another kind of **descriptive writing** is featured in "My Dream Self" on page 53. This activity provides good preparation for writing **personal narratives** and **exploratory essays**.

Help your students' minds roam free by encouraging them to brainstorm as a class, prompting them with questions such as:

- What qualities do you admire?
- Who are some people you look up to?
- What about them wins your respect?
- What do you want to be when you grow up?
- What qualities will you need to do that job?

Encourage your students to write both about the kind of life they'd like to have—"a famous scientist," "an animal trainer," "a ballet dancer"—and about the kind of person they'd like to be —"brave," "disciplined," "someone whom everybody trusts and respects."

THE MOST IMPORTANT DAY . . .

Completing "The Most Important Day..." on page 54 will help your students learn to use specific examples in a **personal narrative**. Get them going by asking about the kinds of days that might be turning points: the day you learned to ride a bike, moved to a new city, made a big mistake that you'll never repeat, took your first big leap off the high dive. Before completing the reproducible, students can brainstorm about important days by using a word web (page 92) or freewriting on a separate sheet of paper.

Name ______________________________ Date ______________

Who I Am

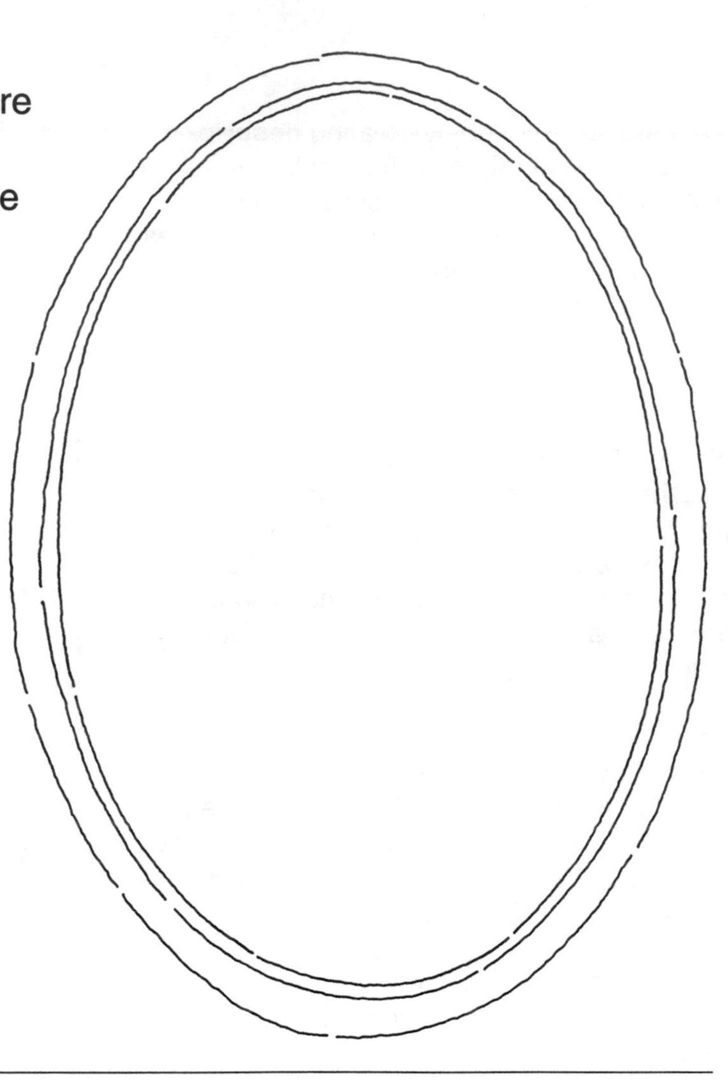

Who are you? Draw a picture of yourself in the mirror. Then describe yourself in the space below. Don't just tell how you look—tell the kind of person you are, too! Here are some things you might want to tell about yourself:

your favorite thing to do

what makes you sad

a dream or wish you have

something you're good at

what you want to do when you grow up

Name ______________________________ Date ______________

My Dream Self

This magic mirror shows you—not the way you are now, but the way you'd like to be someday. What would your dream self be like? Draw a picture in the mirror. Then describe your dream self in the space below.

____

____

____

____

____

____

____

Name ______________________________ Date ______________

The Most Important Day . . .

Think of an event that was very important in your life. It could have been a time that you learned something new, felt something deeply, or made an important decision. Describe what happened and how it affected your life.

____

____

____

____

____

____

____

____

____

The People I Know

Family Treasures

Unlike the other writing activities in this book, "Family Treasures" on page 56 requires some advance preparation. Tell the children in advance to bring in an object that tells about their families—how they are now or how they used to be. Possible objects might include:

- a photograph of the current family
- pictures of relatives when they were young
- an object from another country—an embroidered cloth or a foreign doll

Children might ask family members to share their own memories of the object.

The reproducible offers children two choices: an **essay** about a family artifact, or a **first-person story** from the artifact's point of view. Both encourage students to make use of specific detail and to use time sequencing to order their writing.

Family of the Future

Sometimes children feel freer writing about imaginary families. "Family of the Future" on page 57 lets children write about families in a **science-fiction** mode.

To warm up your future Ray Bradburys and Ursula LeGuins, help children grasp the concept of "100 years." Ask them which of today's inventions didn't exist 100 years ago, and list them on the chalkboard. Next, list their suggestions of how life may be different 100 years from now. Finally, give them the reproducible and let their imaginations take off!

Recipe for a Friend

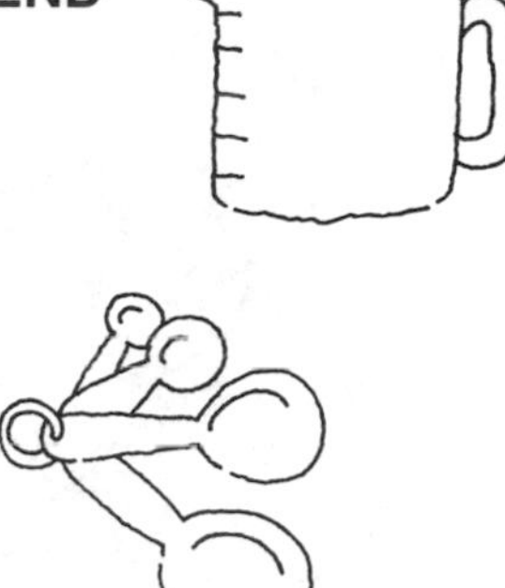

It might be fun to warm up for "Recipe for a Friend" (page 58) by brainstorming the "Ingredients" that make a good friend. For "Directions," you might want to model a sentence or two.

- "Mix friendliness and good sportsmanship. Add a pinch of understanding and a heaping cup of fun."
- "Start with one rainy day. Add a set of marbles, good ideas, and giggles galore."

This playful approach to **how-to writing** will give your students practice in making generalizations and **writing clear directions**.

Desert Island Community

Help your students prepare for "Desert Island Community," the reproducible on page 59, by asking what a person would need on a desert island. Encourage them to think about material things—food, housing, shelter—as well as less tangible needs—amusement, companionship, courage, optimism. Then invite them to think about the types of people who could help them get these things. What skills would they need? What personal qualities should they have? Listing suggestions will help prime your students with concrete ideas for their **expository writing**.

Name ______________________________ Date ______________

Family Treasures

Bring in something from home that's important to you and your family. It could be a photograph of a special time, an object that someone brought from another country, or anything that tells something about you and your history.

Writer's Choice:

1. Describe what you've brought and tell why it's special.

2. Write the story of what you've brought as though the object were telling the story.

Name ____ Date ____________________

FAMILY OF THE FUTURE

It's one hundred years from now. The Futura family is taking a Sunday afternoon drive in their spaceship. Draw a picture of them inside. Then tell who they are and what they are doing.

____

____

____

____

____

____

____

Name ______________________ Date ______________

RECIPE FOR A FRIEND

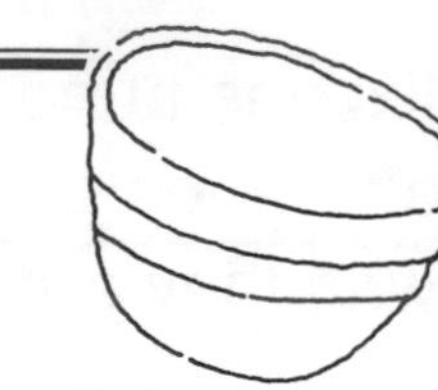

What are the things that make someone a good friend? Use the space below to write a recipe for the ideal friend.

Ingredients

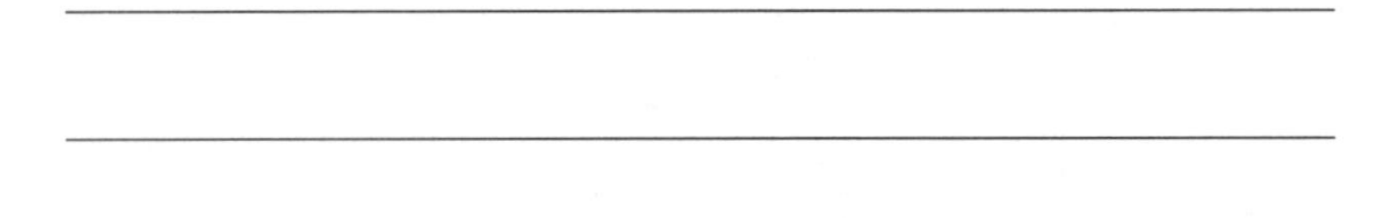

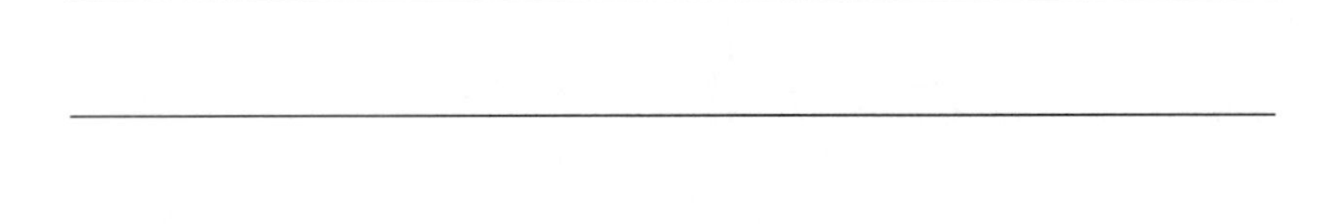
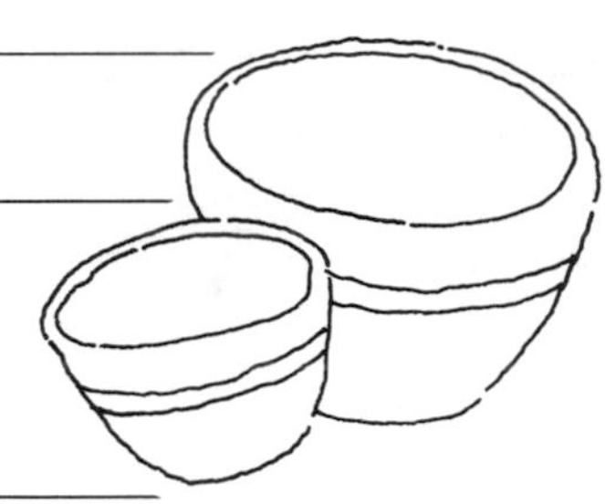

Directions

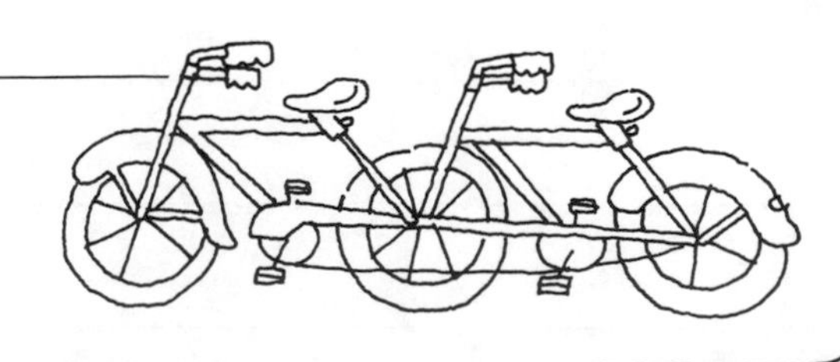

Name ______________________________ Date ______________

Desert Island Community

Suppose you were shipwrecked on a desert island. Whom would you want to have there with you? Tell why you chose that person.

____

____

____

____

____

____

____

NATURE

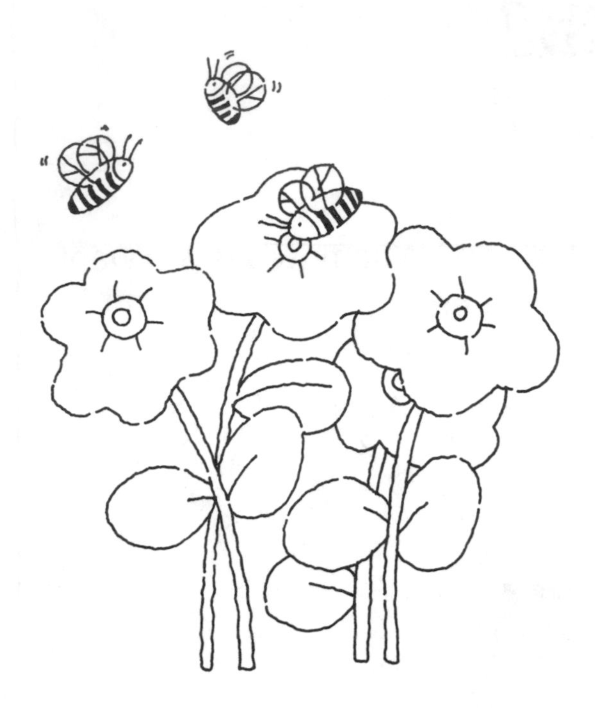

MY FAVORITE PLACE

Children will enjoy the **descriptive writing** of "My Favorite Place," the reproducible on page 61. Help them make their writing full of vivid, sensory images by reminding them of the kinds of words that help writing come alive. You might want to list each of these categories on the chalkboard and invite children to brainstorm examples of each:

- **Words From Our Five Senses**
  blue, green, crash, chirp, rough, silky, sour, perfumed, spicy, sweet
- **Word Pictures** (Similes and Metaphors)
  "an iris as blue as the sky"
  "a butter-yellow sun"
- **Specific Detail**
  "The rocks in the stream bed are pink, brown, and white."
  "In front of the woods is a crumbling brown fence."

Now that your students have reviewed sensory and figurative language, give them the reproducible and let them spend some time in their favorite places!

VISITORS FROM ANOTHER PLANET

"Visitors from Another Planet," the reproducible on page 62, is both a flight of **fantasy** and a chance to write a **travel guide**. You might need to explain that an "itinerary" is a travel plan that lists all the stops on a trip. Children might enjoy seeing real itineraries and tour brochures that you bring in from a local travel agency.

Your students might benefit from a warm-up discussion in which you ask, "What kinds of things would visitors from another planet be interested in? Why?" The ideas they generate can be the building blocks for completing the reproducible. Helping them to focus on their reasons for choosing each stop is a good exercise in using cause-and-effect ordering in their writing; for example, "They would be interested in the ocean *because* they don't have any water on their planet."

Name ______________________________ Date ______________

My Favorite Place

Outside this window is your favorite outdoor place in the whole world. It can be a real place or somewhere you imagine. Draw it, and then describe it on the lines below. Make your description so real that anyone who found this place would recognize it right away!

____

____

____

____

____

____

____

Visitors From Another Planet

Friendly visitors from another planet have chosen you to be their tour guide of Earth. You can take them to places you have been or to places you have only heard about. Where would you take them, and why? Write them a memo outlining their trip. Make your writing vivid so that your visitors will look forward to their tour.

MEMO

Date: ______________________________

To: ______________________________

From: ______________________________

Welcome to planet Earth! I will be your tour guide. This is where we will stop and what we will see.

First Stop: ______________________________

____

Second Stop: ______________________________

____

Third Stop: ______________________________

____

Use the other side if your trip lasts longer than this!

Adventures

A Time Trip

"A Time Trip" on page 64 is a **science-fiction** writing opportunity for your class.

Students might enjoy reading time-travel stories, such as H.G. Wells's *The Time Machine*. Also, Edward Eager's *Half Magic*, *Knight's Castle*, and *The Time Garden* are delightful examples of children's time travel into history.

Save the World!

In "Save the World!" on page 65, children will write a **fantasy**. Help them prepare by introducing the idea that a fantasy is a story that has some elements of reality and others that could not possibly be real. Then invite students to contribute to two lists: "Qualities of a Super Hero" and "Qualities of a Super Villain." Because they'll be writing in the form of a **news story**, build journalism skills by reviewing each of the five W's (who? what? why? where? when?), perhaps using some real news stories as examples.

A Great Invention

A **business letter** full of **expository writing** is called for in "A Great Invention," the reproducible on page 66. You may want to remind students of the elements of a letter: return address and date, salutation and colon, letter body, closing and comma, and signature. You could also review how a business letter differs from a friendly letter. Its purpose may be to obtain or convey information, to make or reply to a request, or to set up a meeting, rather than simply to share news or express affection.

Let your students' minds roam free to invent new gadgets and machines. What about a bed-making machine, a pencil that does all your homework, or a robot that could take your place? Encourage them to write detailed, specific explanations of what their inventions do and how they work.

Adventure Under the Sea

Children might enjoy completing "Adventure Under the Sea" (page 67) after reading other underwater stories, such as Jules Verne's *Twenty Thousand Leagues Under the Sea*. Although they're writing in the form of a **scientific report**, encourage your students to branch out into fantasy if they like, reporting on mermaids and mermen and sea monsters as well as giant squids or killer sharks.

Ride On!

The **adventure story** children write in "Ride On!" (page 68) might be inspired by books such as Robin McKinley's *The Hero and the Crown* or C.S. Lewis's *The Horse and His Boy*. To sharpen story-writing skills, remind students that every good story has a beginning, middle, and an end; includes vivid, lively characters and believable dialogue; and describes *where* and *when* the story takes place.

Name ______________________________ Date ______________

A TIME TRIP

The time machine in the picture is just landing—and you are on it. Where have you gone? Draw a place and time around the time machine—in the future or the past. Then tell what your adventure in time was like.

"When I stepped out of my time machine, ______________________

____

____

____

____

____

____

____

Name ______________________________ Date ______________

SAVE THE WORLD!

POW!

Help! The worst villain in the universe has a terrible plan—and only the strongest super hero alive can save the world. What's the story? Be the reporter who tells the world about the battle of the century—and remember to include the journalist's 5 Ws—Who, What, When, Where, and Why!

AMAZING SUPER HERO WINS BATTLE OF THE CENTURY!

The world was saved this afternoon after an amazing battle between

______________ and ______________. The conflict began when

____

____

____

____

____

____

____

Name ______________________________ Date ______________

A Great Invention

You're a brilliant scientist, and you've just finished your greatest invention. What is it? Draw a picture of it on the lab table. Then describe it in a letter to the head of a company you hope will buy your idea. Tell what it does, how it works, and who will want to use it.

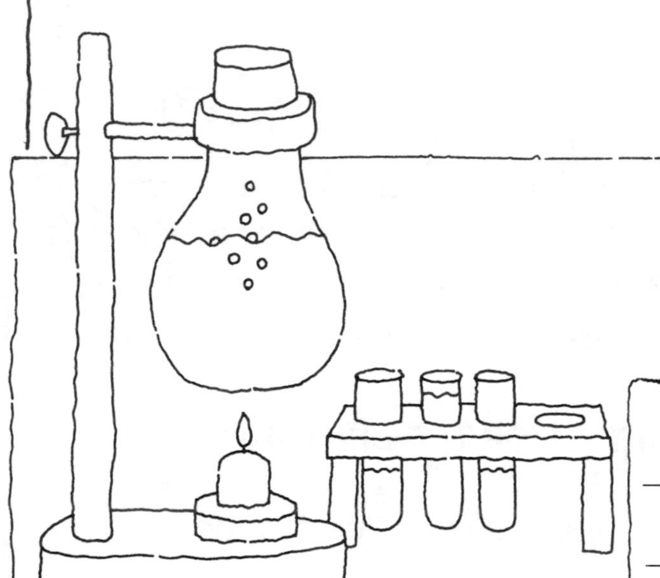

____
(street)

____
(city, state, zip code)

____
(date)

Dear ____________________

____

____

____

____

____

____

Name ______________________________ Date ________________

Adventure Under The Sea

You and your team of underwater scientists are about to land on the ocean floor. What will you see? What will you do? Use the space to draw what you find. Then write a report of your scientific expedition.

Date of Trip: ______________________________

People on Trip: ______________________________

____

Findings: ______________________________

____

____

____

____

____

Conclusion: ______________________________

Name ________________________________ Date ________________

RIDE ON!

The picture shows the fastest, smartest, most skillful horse in the world. Who is riding it, and where are they going? Draw a picture showing a scene from the adventure they are having—then tell the whole story on the lines below.

____

____

____

____

____

____

____

THE WORLD WE LIVE IN

GETTING ALONG

Children can practice their **interview** and **reporting** skills in "Getting Along," the reproducible on page 70. Have partners take turns being the interviewer and the person being interviewed.

Lead into this activity via a general class discussion, inviting children to suggest problems and solutions that involve people getting along with one another.

When children come to interview each other, these tips might be helpful.

For interviewer:

- Ask open-ended questions that can't be answered with "yes" or "no."
- Don't argue with your subject—draw out his or her ideas through discussion.
- Make sure you take careful notes—or test your tape-recording equipment first!

For interviewee:

- Answer questions as fully as you can.
- Give concrete examples when you can.
- Make sure you are speaking clearly and slowly into the microphone if you're using one.

CLEAN UP!

When students write an **editorial** in "Clean Up!" (page 71), they'll be practicing their **persuasive writing** as well. You might start by bringing in some editorials from local, state, and national papers, or by asking them to bring in editorials that they like. Ask them where the opinions in editorials come from, and be sure they understand that editorials reflect the point of view of a newspaper's editorial board.

When students actually start writing, suggest that they list their ideas in order of importance, building their **sequencing** skills. Encourage them to think about who will read their editorial—each other, parents, other adults—to sharpen their audience awareness.

Your class might publish their work in a class paper—or submit their work to school, local, or national student publications.

IF I WERE IN CHARGE. . .

Before they write their **campaign speeches** for "If I Were in Charge. . . " (page 72), remind students of the elements of a good speech:

- It takes account of its audience's thoughts, feelings, and expectations.
- It starts with an interesting lead that lets the audience know what the speech will be about.
- It is clear and direct.
- Its ideas are in some kind of order, such as order of importance.

Students might have fun giving their speeches to small groups or to the class. You might even want to organize "elections" for "community boss"!

LETTER TO THE EDITOR

"Letter to the Editor" on page 73 combines **letter writing** with **persuasive writing** skills. If necessary, review letter format with your students. They might enjoy reading some real letters to the editor and talking about which are effective and why.

Encourage students to pick a topic they feel strongly about and to submit their letters for publication!

Name ______________________________ Date ______________

GETTING ALONG

Write four questions to ask a partner about why people don't always get along and what we can do about it. Write down your partner's answers in the spaces provided.

QUESTION: ______________________________

ANSWER: ______________________________

____

QUESTION: ______________________________

ANSWER: ______________________________

____

QUESTION: ______________________________

ANSWER: ______________________________

____

QUESTION: ______________________________

ANSWER: ______________________________

____

Ask your partner each question. Tape-record his or her answers, if possible. Write down the answers, as well. You may want to re-create your interview for your class.

Name ______________________________ Date ______________

Clean Up!

Our world is getting dirty. What can we do to clean it up? Draw a picture of one pollution problem you think we have today. Then, in the space below, write an editorial about how you think we could clean it up.

____

____

____

____

____

____

Name ______________________________ Date ______________

If I Were In Charge . . .

Have you always wished you could make some changes in your neighborhood or community? Well, now's your chance! What would you do if *you* were in charge? Write your speech in the space below, telling what changes you would make and why.

Name ______________________________ Date ______________

LETTER TO THE EDITOR

Choose one thing about the world you live in that you think should change. It could be something in your neighborhood, your city, the country, or the whole world. Then write a letter to the editor of a newspaper saying what should change, why, and how.

____
(date)

To the Editor: ______________________________

Imaginary Worlds

Children enjoy creating special play worlds for themselves. The reproducibles on pages 75-77 offer opportunities to expand these worlds through writing.

On My Planet

Children get to stretch their imaginations as they write a **free-verse poem** for "On My Planet," the reproducible on page 75. Remind your young poets that free verse gives them the freedom to find their own rhythms, as they choose just the right length for each line. Sharing some free-verse poetry, such as work by Langston Hughes, Alice Walker, or e.e. cummings, can help your students see some of the expressive possibilities in this kind of writing. Asking students how the poems make them feel might start off a useful lead-in discussion to the writing activity.

Picture This!

Children can choose the form their **fantasy** will take in "Picture This!," the reproducible on page 76. Working with others in a small group, they can imagine the rules of a magic land and translate their thoughts into an adventure story. Explaining how things work in this magic land will sharpen their explanatory skills and hone their imaginations.

It's a Silly World!

Children can choose their genre in "It's a Silly World," the reproducible on page 77. This **fantasy** about a world in which everything is backwards, upside down, or just plain silly can take the form of a **news article**, a **short story**, or a **description**. Children may draw on their skill with vivid language as well as their senses of humor as they complete this playful activity in small writing groups.

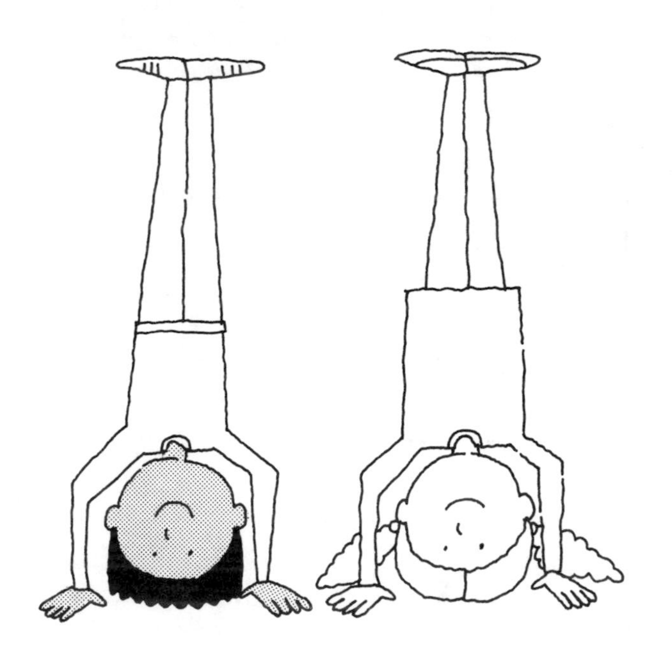

Name ______________________________ Date ______________

ON MY PLANET

The planet in the picture is *your* own world. What happens there is up to you. Fill in some of the details in the picture. Then write a free-verse poem about what life is like on your planet.

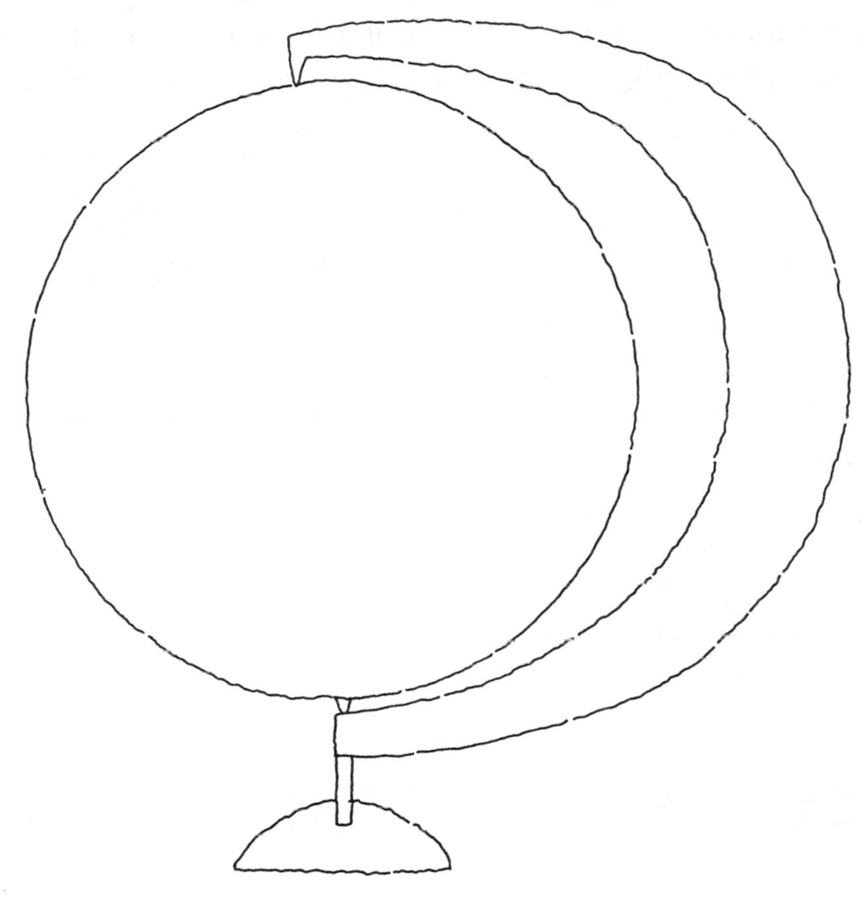

____

____

____

____

____

____

____

Name ______________________________ Date ______________

Picture This!

Have you ever looked at a picture and pretended to step into it? Imagine that you and the members of your small group are sailing off to a land of adventure. Work out together where you are going and what kind of adventures you might have there. Draw yourselves and your companions on the ship. Then, in the space below, work together to describe your adventures.

____

____

____

____

____

____

____

Name ______________________________ Date ______________

It's A Silly World!

Can you imagine a world in which *nothing* works the same as it does in this one?... a very silly world in which *everything* is ridiculous and *nothing* makes sense? Brainstorm about this world with your group. Then tell about your ideas in the space below. Write a short story, a news article, a description, or any other kind of piece that tells about your silly world.

Word Games

What kind of dog can tell time?

A watch dog!

The word play in the reproducibles on pages 79-81 offers your students a chance to sharpen their **word choice** and **vocabulary skills**, and to build a feeling for the sounds of words.

The Same and Different

If necessary, go over the concepts of **synonyms** and **antonyms** with students before they begin "The Same and Different" (page 79). Playing with synonyms and antonyms will help students compare and contrast elements in their writing, as well as build cooperative writing skills as they work with their partners.

Pun Fun and Riddle Games

Children might enjoy hearing or reading the nonsense poetry of Edward Lear or Lewis Carroll, or the playful verse of e.e. cummings or James Berry to warm them up for "Pun Fun and Riddle Games" (page 80). If your students have joke or riddles to contribute, invite them to share the fun!

Then make sure that students understand that the answers to many riddles are puns, or plays on words. Remind them that for the writing activity, they and their partners are to invent *new* riddles—otherwise, their classmates might have heard them before!

Tall Tales

One of the best ways of teaching **hyperbole** is to let students write **tall tales**, as they get to do in "Tall Tales," the reproducible on page 81. You might lead into the activity by inviting students to read or retell such tall tales as the stories of Paul Bunyan or John Henry. Help students identify what makes tall tales "tall"—the exaggeration and hyperbole that couldn't possibly be real but makes its point. ("He ran faster than a bolt of lightning." "She moved at a snail's pace.") You might want to encourage students to model some hyperboles about larger-than-life characters from literature, TV, or the movies before setting them loose to work on the reproducible. (Troll's *American Folk Heroes* series includes the tales of John Henry, Mike Fink, Paul Bunyan, Pecos Bill, and more.)

Name ______________________________ Date ______________

The Same And Different

Some words are **synonyms**—they mean the same thing. The words "happy" and "glad" are synonyms. Other words are about differences. They're called **antonyms**, and they mean opposite things. The words "happy" and "sad" are antonyms. Work with a partner to come up with three pairs of synonyms and three pairs of antonyms. Write them on the lines below.

Synonyms		**Antonyms**	
______	______	______	______
______	______	______	______
______	______	______	______

Now work with your partner to write a story about two very similar characters who meet a pair of "opposites." Use as many synonyms and antonyms as you can. Continue the story on the back of the page, if necessary.

____

____

____

____

____

Name ______________________________ Date ______________

PUN FUN AND RIDDLE GAMES

"What's black and white and red (read) all over?"

"How does a piano work?"

"What did the court jester say when the king locked him up for making bad jokes?"

If you want to find the answers, look at the bottom of the page!

These riddles work because of *puns*—plays on words. Work with a partner to invent some riddles and puns of your own. Write your word games on the lines below. Then share them with another writing team. And remember—have pun!

____

____

____

____

____

"A newspaper!" "It doesn't work—it plays!" "Oh, pun the door!"

Name ______________________________ Date ______________

TALL TALES

How would you describe someone who's really big?... If you said the person was "bigger than a building," you would be exaggerating, but you would get your point across. Write three descriptive sentences, using exaggeration to make your point. You can describe the character in the picture or make up people of your own.

______________ was so thin, he ______________________.

______________ was so fast, it ______________________.

______________ was so slow, it ______________________.

Now write a tall tale, telling about the adventures of one of these characters. Remember, in a tall tale, everything is exaggerated! (If you need more space, use the back of this page.)

____

____

____

____

TELLING TALES

The reproducibles on pages 83-85 will introduce your students to the elements of **short stories—characters**, **plot**, **setting**; **conflict**, **climax**, **resolution**. Your students can also use Cynthia Rylant's wonderful **short story**, "Slower Than the Rest," from her collection, *Every Living Thing*, as a model for their own writing.

Start by inviting students to bring in their own favorite books and stories to share. (You may want to allow TV and movie stories, too.)

LISTEN AND WRITE

Cynthia Rylant's "Slower Than the Rest" portrays a well-drawn **character** facing a **conflict** and achieving **resolution**. You might either read the story aloud or ask students to do so; or you might prefer to let students read the story on their own. In any case, help students notice how Rylant establishes her main character (Leo), his conflict (he is unhappy about being considered "slower than the rest"), and his resolution (he performs well in a school activity about forest fires). Then invite your students to complete "Listen and Write," the reproducible on page 83. They may want to share their short stories with each other, or to take more class time to develop their stories.

CHARACTERS, PLOT, SETTING

Get your class thinking about a story's major elements—**characters**, **plot**, and **setting**—by encouraging someone to retell a story the whole class knows. Then ask students to identify the story's characters, plot, and setting.

You may also want to use "Slower Than the Rest" for this activity, or you might read through several stories in *Every Living Thing* with the class until you're sure students have grasped the concept. (Character is especially important in "Retired" and "A Pet." "Drying Out" and "Stray" offer particularly interesting plots. Setting is a key element in "Boar Out There" and "Papa's Parrot.")

Now hand out the **Listen and Write** reproducible. Children will use this page to create characters they would like to write about. Remember to allow more class time for them to actually write the stories they've begun to plan.

CONFLICT, CLIMAX, RESOLUTION

Your students can grasp the **mechanics of a story** by completing "Conflict, Climax, Resolution," the reproducible on page 85. Invite the class to suggest familiar stories, or use examples from *Every Living Thing*. Walk students through an analysis of these elements in each story.

When students have gotten the idea, give them the reproducible and encourage them to use it to plan a story of their own. You may want to give them some more class time to complete their stories. It's often helpful to take a day or more between writing a first draft and revising.

Collaborative writing hint: Some students like to talk through their ideas with a writing partner before actually setting pencil to paper.

Name ______________________________ Date ______________

LISTEN AND WRITE

Listen to your teacher reading aloud "Slower Than the Rest" from Cynthia Rylant's book, *Every Living Thing*. Notice how Rylant helps you picture the type of person that Leo is, tells you what his main problem is, and then tells you something he did that helped him solve his problem. Then create a character *you* would like to write about. Write about a problem this person has and a way that he or she finds to solve the problem. If you need more room, use the other side of this page.

____

____

____

____

____

____

____

____

____

Name ______________________________ Date ______________

Characters, Plot, Setting

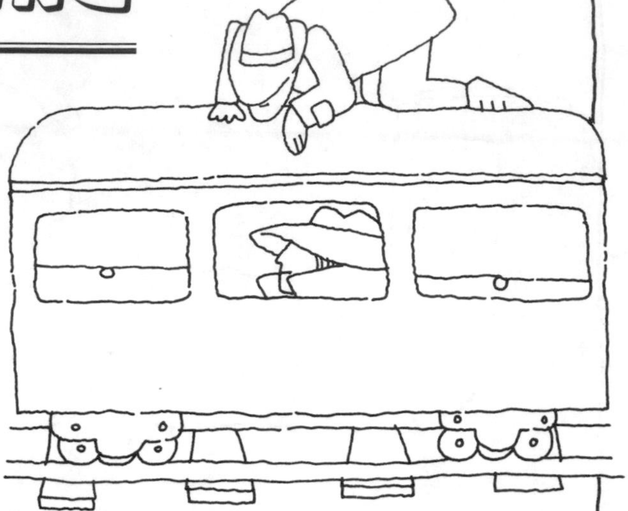

What are the elements of a story?

Characters—who the story is about.

Setting—when and where the story takes place.

Plot—what the story is about.

Start cooking up a story of your own. Think of a tale you'd like to tell, and complete the sentences below.

The characters in my story are ______________________________

____

The time when my story takes place is ______________________________

____

The place where my story is set is ______________________________

____

This is what my story is about: ______________________________

____

Name ______________________________ Date ______________

Conflict, Climax, Resolution

How do you create a good story? Once you know about your characters, setting, and plot, you move on to your **conflict**—a problem that happens in the plot of a story. When the conflict moves to its most exciting point, that's the story's **climax**. And when the story's problem is solved, that's the **resolution**.

Think of a story you'd like to tell using your notes from **characters, plot, setting**. Then complete these sentences.

The conflict in my story is between ____________ and ______________.

The climax is ____

____.

The resolution is ____

____.

Now use the other side of this page to write the first draft of your story. Then come back to your story and revise it, until it's the best story it can be!

Diaries And Journals

Keeping a **diary** or a **journal** is an excellent way for your students to write freely and fluidly about any topic that interests them. **Diaries**, of course, are for thoughts and feelings; **journals** or logs include note-taking, planning new projects, and reactions to events, observations, and sometimes feelings as well.

If you'd like your students to keep a **journal**, we recommend encouraging them to buy a separate journal notebook, giving them the most flexibility in including the range of writing activities suitable for that form. Students might write in their journals every day, during designated class time, or as the spirit moves them. You might want to use the following brainstorming questions to help get your students into the journal-writing spirit:

- What new projects would I like to start?
- What did I notice today that I'd like to remember?
- Did I feel strongly about something today? What was it? How would I describe my feelings?
- Today, I realized that ______________.
- Today, I wondered whether ___________.

Dear Diary

To encourage your students' **diary** writing, give each student several copies of "Dear Diary," the reproducible on page 87, and let them bind their work together with yarn, string, or brass fasteners. You might also want to provide covers of oaktag or construction paper for them to decorate.

You might model a **diary entry** or two of your own to help students see how free they can feel to express their thoughts and feelings.

Writer's Choice

In "Writer's Choice," the reproducible on page 88, your young writers get to choose their own topics, as well as their own formats and genres. You might encourage them to keep a running list of topic ideas in their journals, so that when they get a "writer's choice," they'll have some ideas ready-made.

Name ______________________________ Date ______________

DEAR DIARY

MY DIARY

PRIVATE DIARY OF ...

Dear Diary:

Name ______________________________ Date ______________

WRITER'S CHOICE

What would you like to write about? This page is for you—write anything you like. Here are some suggestions to get your thinking going, but feel free to choose something completely different. You can also use the space to write a poem or a play.

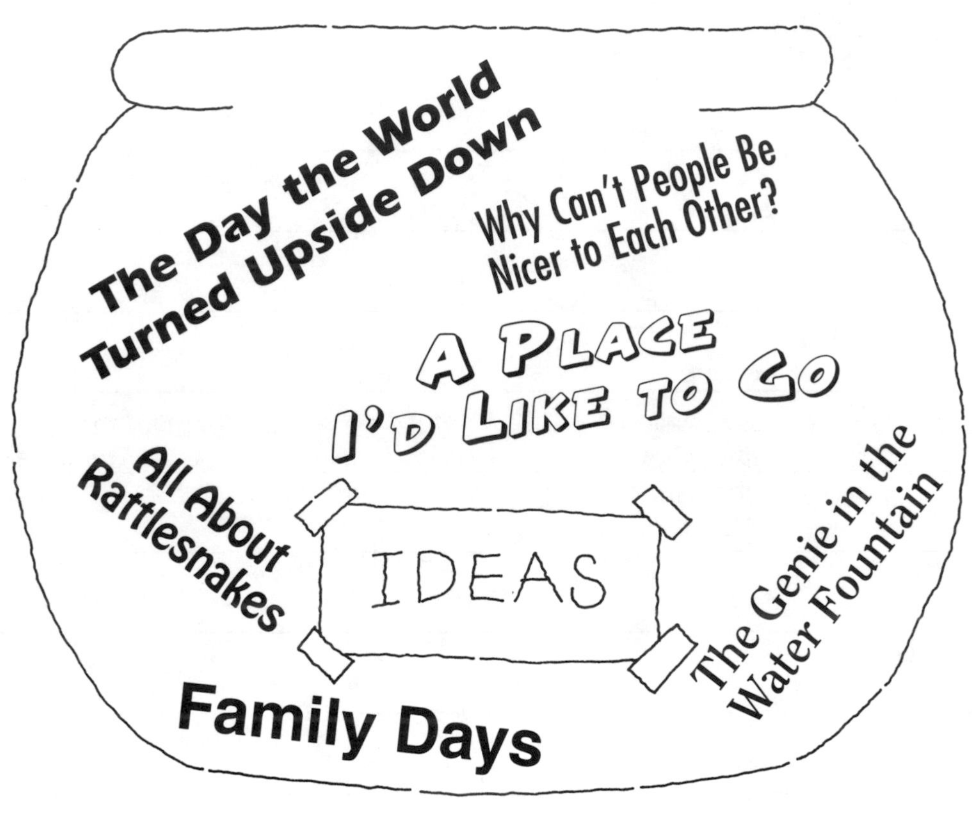

____

____

____

____

____

____

____

How to Use the Appendix

This Appendix includes a number of all-purpose writing aids that you might find helpful. These models can be posted on the bulletin board, displayed on the overhead projector, or duplicated and distributed to your students.

"The Writing Process at a Glance" (page 90) is designed for students who are already familiar with the five steps of the writing process: brainstorming, organizing, drafting, editing/revising/proofreading, and sharing. The page can serve as a reminder posted on the bulletin board, or as a checklist for students to refer to each time they move through the writing process.

"Brainstorming Questions" (page 91) is a reminder for children who understand the concept of brainstorming but who could use some help getting started. You might want to use the sheet as is, or excerpt the portions that relate to the type of writing your class is doing at the moment.

"Word Web" (page 92), "Idea Flow Chart" (page 93), and "Sample Outline" (page 94) can be distributed by you for children to use in their brainstorming and organizing. Or you might want to post them in some visible place as a reminder for students to create similar aids on their own.

"Planning a Story" (page 95) is a quick reminder of story structure for children already familiar with this concept (see the sections "Story Time," pages 39-43, and "Telling Tales," pages 82-85). By answering these questions, students will discover that they've generated all the elements they need to write a complete and satisfying story.

Finally, the "Cut-Apart Organizer" (page 96) is an excellent way to familiarize students with the notion of index cards. Allow students to write their thoughts on the organizer, then cut the cards apart and reshuffle them at will. Some students will want to stack the cards, others will prefer to spread them out on their desks in different patterns. Whatever they choose, students will be working to develop the organizational strategies that are right for them.

Students at all levels can use most of the aids in the Appendix, although "The Writing Process at a Glance," "Brainstorming Questions," and "Planning a Story" are probably more useful for older or advanced students.

As with everything else in this book, the Appendix is here for your convenience, to use in whatever way is most effective in your classroom. Feel free to adapt or change anything here to suit your needs and those of your students.

The Writing Process At A Glance

1. Brainstorming

What will you write about? What do you want to say? This is the time to come up with lots of ideas!

Let your mind run free! Jot down everything you think of.

Some ways to brainstorm:

- lists
- mind map
- talking with a partner
- freewriting
- talking with a small group

2. Organizing

Put your ideas in order *before* you start writing. What's the main idea? Which supporting details make the main idea clear? Which ideas don't belong?

Some ways to organize:

- outline
- diagram
- word web
- cut-and-paste organizer
- note cards
- Venn diagram

3. Drafting

Finally it's time to put your ideas into sentences and paragraphs. Say what you mean as clearly as you can.

Hints for drafting:

- Pretend you are talking to a friend. What would you say? Write it down!
- Don't worry about making mistakes. You can correct them later.

4. Editing, Revising, and Proofreading

Take a look at what you wrote. (You might like to take a break first.) Did you say what you meant? Is your writing the best it can be? Are your grammar, spelling, and punctuation correct? This is your chance to make changes and improvements.

Some things to watch for in editing and revising:

- ideas that don't belong
- missing information
- words that aren't clear
- images that aren't vivid

Some things to watch for in proofreading:

- capital letters
- spelling
- periods
- commas

5. Sharing

Remember that what you have written is for an audience. Sharing can take the form of simply showing or reading your writing to a friend, submitting it to a school magazine, or posting it on a class bulletin board. (Some writing, a diary entry for example, is just for yourself. Then *you* are the audience.)

Brainstorming Questions

Get your mind in gear! Here are some questions that might help your ideas start flowing.

For Reports

- Why is this topic important to me?
- If I were reading this report, what would I want to know?
- What do I know already?
- What do I want to find out?

For Letters

- If I had the person here, what would I say?
- If I were getting this letter, what would I want to read?

For How-To Writing

- Why do people need to know how to do this?
- I'm picturing someone who doesn't know how to do this. If that person were right here, what would I say?
- What was easy for me to learn?
- What was hard for me to learn?

For Stories

- Who's my main character?
- What's the problem my main character has to solve?
- If I met my main character at school, what would I notice?
- What interesting things might happen to my character?
- How does my character feel?
- How does my character solve his or her problem?
- Where and when does my story take place?

WORD WEB

Need some help getting started? Use this word web to help you brainstorm. Write your main topic in the big center circle. Write your subtopics in the circles around the main topic. Then fill the small outer circles with ideas that "spin off" from your subtopics.

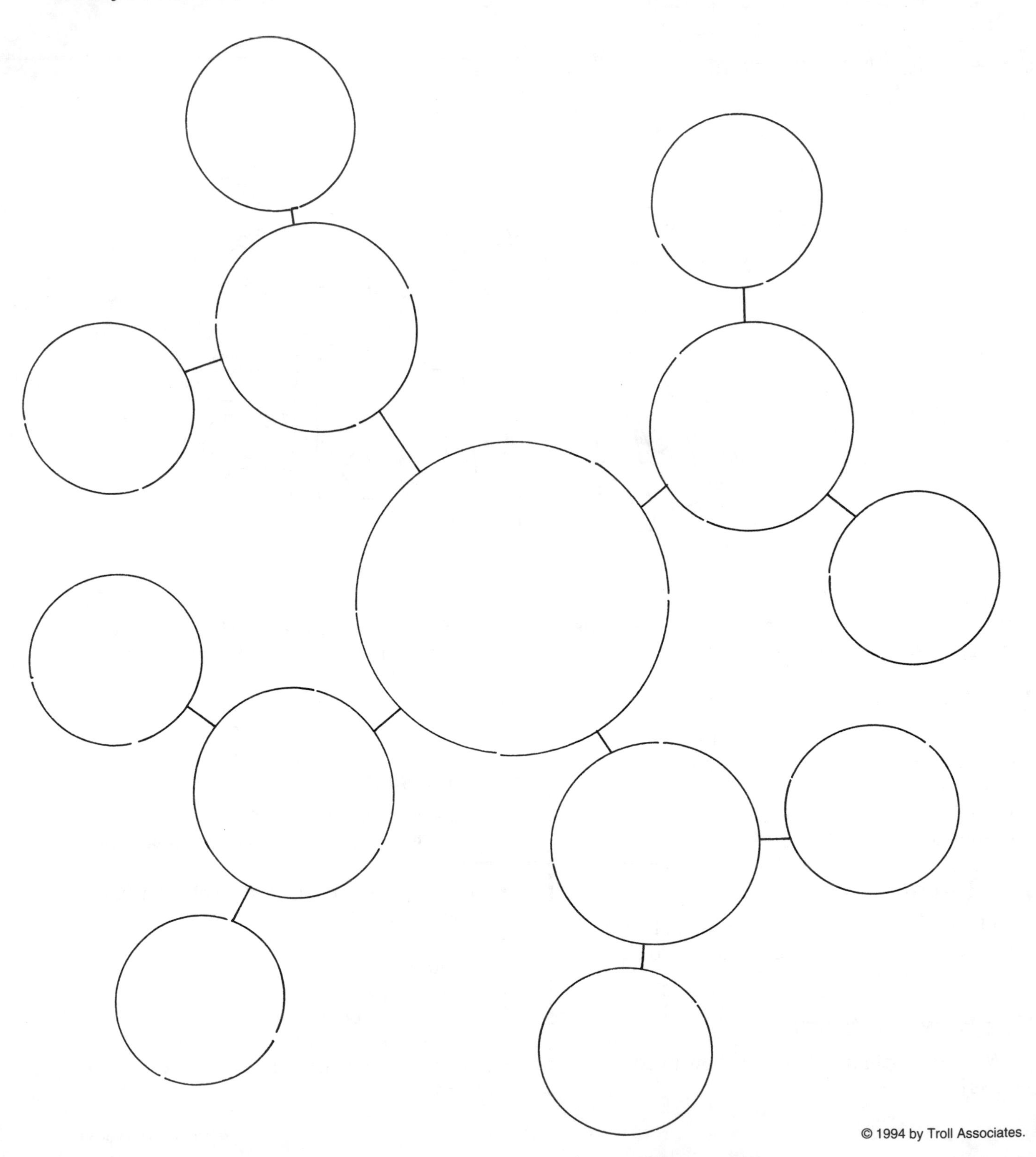

IDEA FLOW CHART

Do you want your ideas to flow freely? This flow chart might help! Write your starting idea in the first box. Fill each of the other boxes with ideas that flow from the previous one.

START

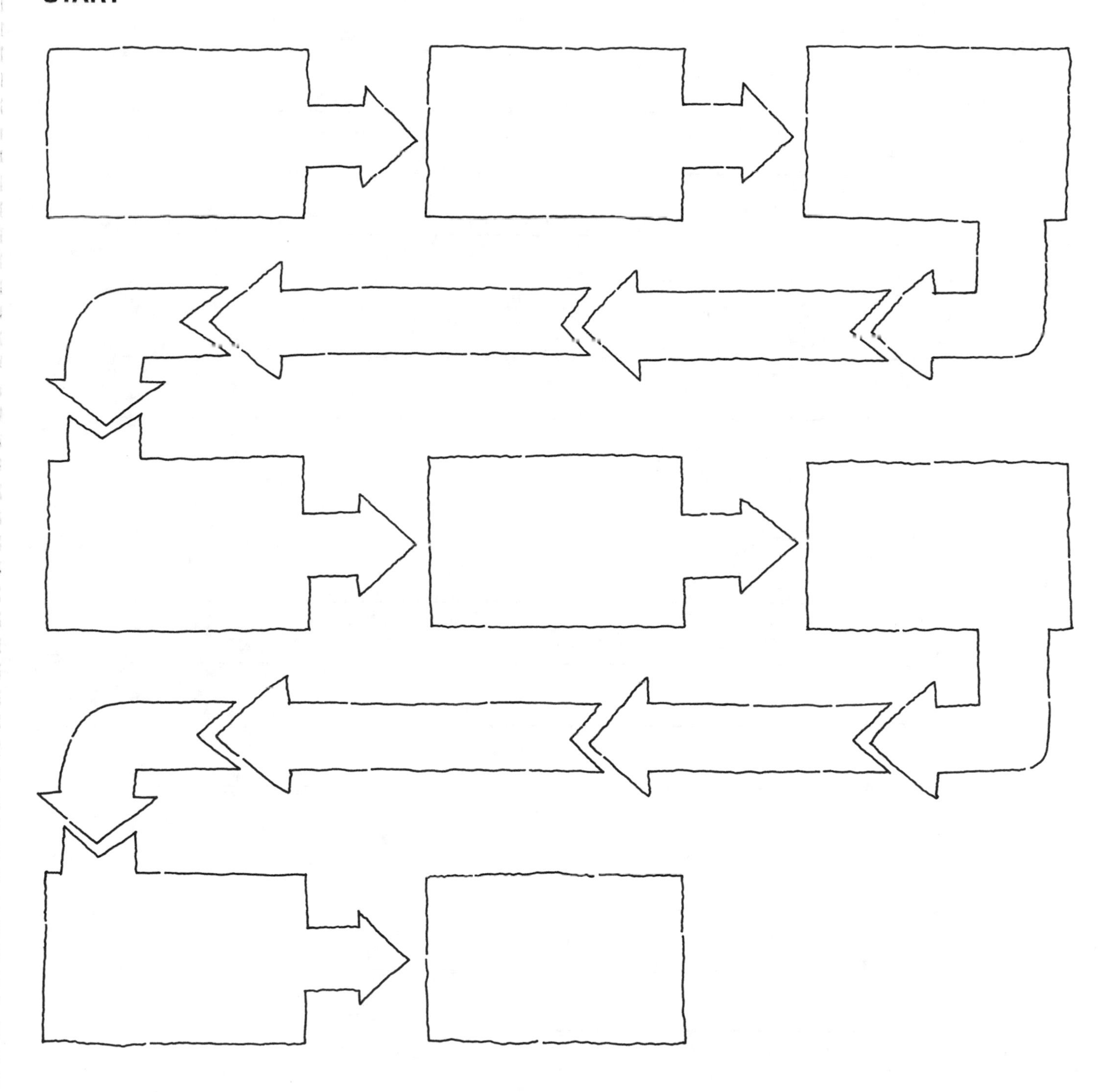

SAMPLE OUTLINE

Getting your ideas in order? This sample outline will help.

Title ______________________________

I. ______________________________

A. ______________________________

1. ______________________________

2. ______________________________

B. ______________________________

1. ______________________________

2. ______________________________

II. ______________________________

A. ______________________________

1. ______________________________

2. ______________________________

B. ______________________________

1. ______________________________

2. ______________________________

Planning A Story

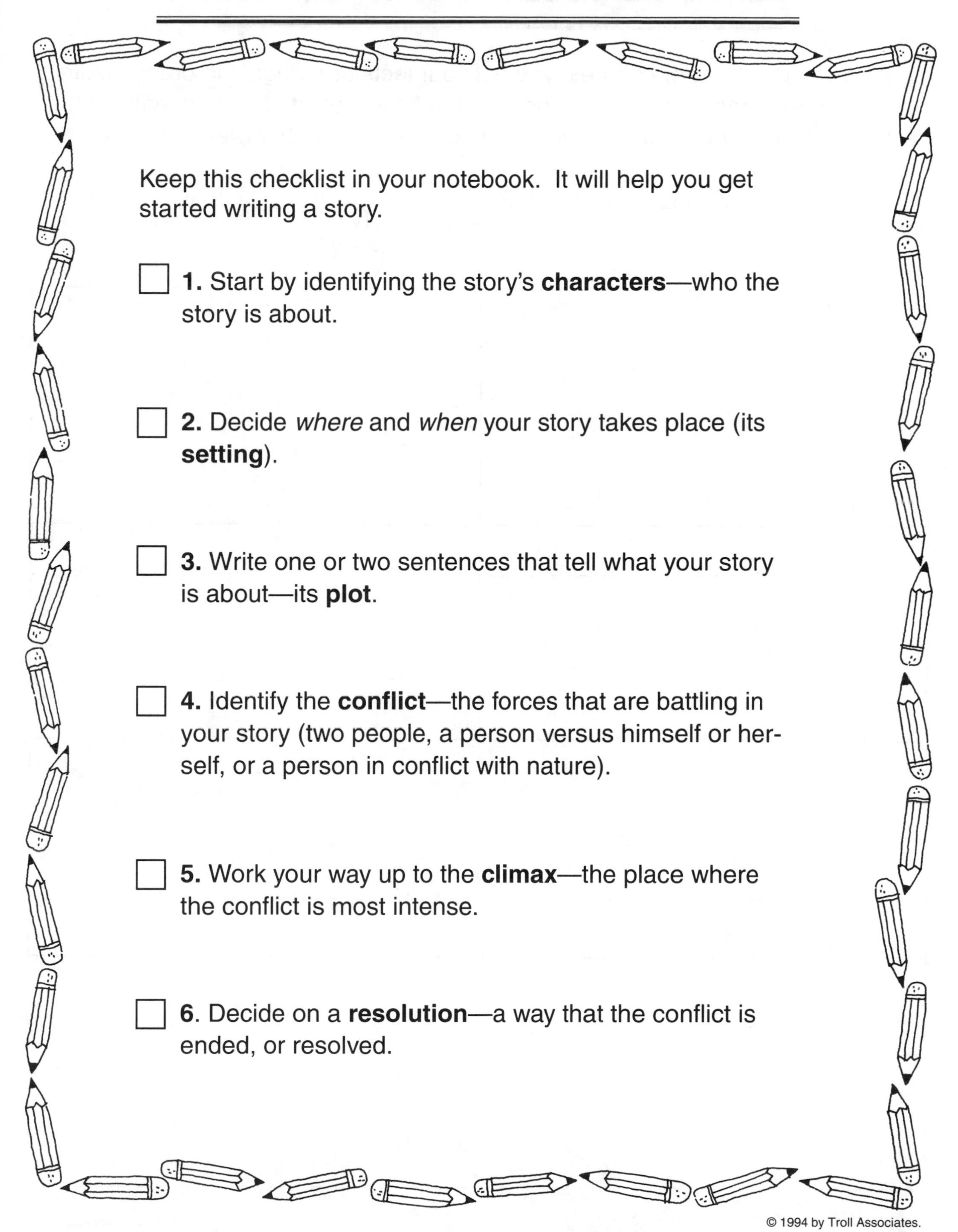

Keep this checklist in your notebook. It will help you get started writing a story.

- ☐ **1.** Start by identifying the story's **characters**—who the story is about.

- ☐ **2.** Decide *where* and *when* your story takes place (its **setting**).

- ☐ **3.** Write one or two sentences that tell what your story is about—its **plot**.

- ☐ **4.** Identify the **conflict**—the forces that are battling in your story (two people, a person versus himself or herself, or a person in conflict with nature).

- ☐ **5.** Work your way up to the **climax**—the place where the conflict is most intense.

- ☐ **6**. Decide on a **resolution**—a way that the conflict is ended, or resolved.

CUT-APART ORGANIZER

This cut-apart organizer can help you get your facts or thoughts in order. Write one fact or thought in each box. Then cut the boxes apart. Mix and match, shuffle and re-shuffle, until you've got your ideas in just the right order!

You can make more boxes of your own.

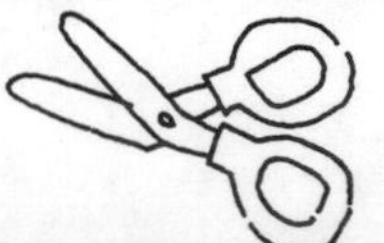